Understanding

The Yearling

New and future titles in the Understanding Great Literature
series include:

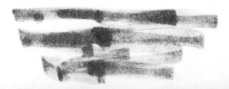

Understanding

The Yearling

UNDERSTANDING GREAT LITERATURE

Jennifer Keeley

Lucent Books
P.O. Box 289011
San Diego, CA 92198-9011

On cover: Marjorie Kinnan Rawlings, author of *The Yearling.*

Library of Congress Cataloging-in-Publication Data

Keeley, Jennifer, 1974–
    The yearling / by Jennifer Keeley
        p. cm. — (Understanding great literature)
Includes biographical references (p.) and index.
Summary: Discusses the novel, "The Yearling," including the life
of Marjorie Kinnan Rawlings Baskin, the book's history and
impact, its plot, characters, and literary criticism.
    ISBN 1-56006-811-6 (alk. paper)
    1. Rawlings, Marjorie Kinnan, 1896–1953. Yearling. 2.
Human-animal relationships in literature. 3. Parent and child in
literature. 4. Florida—In literature. 5. Deer in literature. 6. Boys
in literature. [1. Rawlings, Marjorie Kinnan, 1896–1953.
Yearling. 2. American literature—History and criticism.] I. Title.
II. Series.
    PS3535.A845 Y35 2001
    813'.52—dc21

00-008755

Contents

FOREWORD

"Except for a living man, there is nothing more wonderful than a book!" wrote the widely respected nineteenth-century teacher and writer Charles Kingsley. A book, he continued, "is a message to us from human souls we never saw. And yet these [books] arouse us, terrify us, teach us, comfort us, open our hearts to us as brothers." There are many different kinds of books, of course; and Kingsley was referring mainly to those containing literature—novels, plays, short stories, poems, and so on. In particular, he had in mind those works of literature that were and remain widely popular with readers of all ages and from many walks of life.

Such popularity might be based on one or several factors. On the one hand, a book might be read and studied by people in generation after generation because it is a literary classic, with characters and themes of universal relevance and appeal. Homer's epic poems, the *Iliad* and the *Odyssey*, Chaucer's *Canterbury Tales*, Shakespeare's *Hamlet* and *Romeo and Juliet*, and Dickens's *A Christmas Carol* fall into this category. Some popular books, on the other hand, are more controversial. Mark Twain's *Huckleberry Finn* and J. D. Salinger's *The Catcher in the Rye*, for instance, have their legions of devoted fans who see them as great literature; while others view them as less than worthy because of their racial depictions, profanity, or other factors.

Still another category of popular literature includes realistic modern fiction, including novels such as Robert Cormier's *I Am the Cheese* and S. E. Hinton's *The Outsiders*. Their keen social insights and sharp character portrayals have consistently reached out to and captured the imaginations of many teenagers and young adults; and for this reason they are often assigned and studied in schools.

These and other similar works have become the "old standards" of the literary scene. They are the ones that people most often read, discuss, and study; and each has, by virtue of its content, critical success, or just plain longevity, earned the right to be the subject of a book examining its content. (Some, of course, like the *Iliad* and *Hamlet*, have been the subjects of numerous books already; but their literary stature is so lofty that there can never be too many books about them!) For millions of readers and students in one generation after another, each of these works becomes, in a sense, an adventure in appreciation, enjoyment, and learning.

The main purpose of Lucent's Understanding Great Literature series is to aid the reader in that ongoing literary adventure. Each volume in the series focuses on a single literary work that a majority of critics and teachers view as a classic and/or that is widely studied and discussed in schools. A typical volume first tells why the work in question is important. Then follow detailed overviews of the author's life, the work's historical background, its plot, its characters, and its themes. Numerous quotes from the work, as well as by critics and other experts, are interspersed throughout and carefully documented with footnotes for those who wish to pursue further research. Also included is a list of ideas for essays and other student projects relating to the work, an appendix of literary criticisms and analyses by noted scholars, and a comprehensive annotated bibliography.

The great nineteenth-century American poet Henry David Thoreau once quipped: "Read the best books first, or you may not have a chance to read them at all." For those who are reading or about to read the "best books" in the literary canon, the comprehensive, thorough, and thoughtful volumes of the Understanding Great Literature series are indispensable guides and sources of enrichment.

INTRODUCTION

The Yearling Experience

The *Yearling* was published in 1938 and became an undisputed success. The story of Jody Baxter and his pet fawn, Flag, quickly rocketed to the top of best-seller lists, selling more than a quarter of a million copies in its first year, and remained on top for nearly two years. It also achieved critical success. Reviewers raved about the story and its craftsmanship, boldly declaring that someday it would be considered an American classic. In 1939, this prophecy seemed as though it was destined to come true when the book was awarded the Pulitzer Prize in fiction.

However, the passage of time has not necessarily been kind to Marjorie Kinnan Rawlings's classic. In the years since its publication, various critics and academics have questioned the book's literary and artistic value. W. J. Stuckey argues that *The Yearling* is "too slight and sentimental to merit serious [critical] attention" and adds that "Mrs. Rawlings' writing is generally amateurish."[1] Even some of Rawlings's fiercest advocates, such as Gordon E. Bigelow, are forced to confess that her "gift was not a major one like [William] Faulkner's" and that she may have owed a good portion of her initial popular success to "the tom-toms of press agentry."[2]

Yet despite critics' claims about the book's "artistic defects" and sentimentality, thousands of copies of *The Yearling* are still sold every year, now more than half a century after its initial publication. Reviewers maintain that the book continues to enjoy widespread popularity because it is a well-written, touching story that introduces readers to both an uplifting ideology and a unique world. Early reviewers focused on the beauty and tenderness of Jody Baxter's coming of age. "There comes a moment everywhere when ceasing to be a boy may be a tragedy like dying," wrote Jonathan Daniels in his review of *The Yearling* for the *Saturday Review of Literature.* "But the story of that moment has never been more tenderly written than by Marjorie Kinnan Rawlings."[3] Edith H. Walton seconded this in the *New York Times Book Review,* telling readers that *The Yearling* "casts with unusual beauty the old, timeless story of youth's growth to maturity."[4]

While some critics find the book touching, others point to the characters, especially Jody Baxter, when looking to explain the book's popularity. William Soskin boldly declared Jody "the most charming boy"[5] in American literature, and over the years numerous critics have joined in praising the characters

Rawlings's book, The Yearling, *was such a success that a film of the same name was produced in 1946.*

and arguing they are the key to the book's success. Bigelow cites them as "one reason for *The Yearling*'s excellence as fiction"[6] and Samuel I. Bellman asserts that Rawlings's sympathetic writing of Jody Baxter is "the most important reason that *The Yearling* maintains so strong a hold on the reader."[7]

The characters also provide the reader with a glimpse into their unique world, the nineteenth-century Florida scrub. This tribute to a time and place that has long since vanished is further enhanced by the timelessness of the emotions Rawlings conveys. According to Rodger L. Tarr, this is one reason Rawlings's works sell, "because they are enduring records of time past and present."[8]

Not only does *The Yearling* present readers with incredible characters and exotic settings, it also conveys a powerful ideology. Critic Christine McDonnell realized this in her second reading of the book. Having read it as a child, she was pleasantly surprised as an adult to find herself fascinated by "the view of life that Marjorie Kinnan Rawlings reveals." McDonnell concludes the book is worth a "second look" because it shows the reader how powerful it is "to come to terms with the duality of life, the pain and the joy, and to learn to believe in your own strength and endurance, and . . . to realize the suffering of each man and to see it as something linked to your own."[9]

Thus, *The Yearling* offers readers touching moments, believable characters, beautiful natural settings, and an uplifting ideology. However, none of these could be enjoyed without actually reading the novel. One of the most important keys to the book's popularity may very well be that it is a page-turner, a good read. This left Bigelow to conclude that the book—and all of Rawlings's works—has "the important virtue of readability." He went on to defend the author against her numerous critics, arguing simply that Rawlings "will probably continue to be more a reader's writer than a critic's writer since the special virtues of her books are more readily experienced than described."[10] This book is about that experience.

CHAPTER ONE

The Life of Marjorie Kinnan Rawlings

Marjorie Kinnan was born to Ida and Arthur Frank Kinnan on August 8, 1896. She was the first of two Kinnan children; her brother, Arthur Houston Kinnan, would come into the world four years later. Since Arthur Kinnan was an examiner for the U.S. Patent Office, the family lived in a suburb of Washington, D.C., called Brookland.

Marjorie's father also owned a small dairy farm just ten miles away from the family home. In the evenings and on weekends he loved to work the farm. Marjorie shared a very special relationship with her father, and it was from him that she first learned to observe and appreciate nature.

As an adult, Rawlings was admired for both her ability to write eloquently about nature and her storytelling. Thus, it is not surprising that just as she developed her love of nature as a youngster, so too did she begin to tell stories. Years later Rawlings recalled,

> Spring and summer nights . . . I sat on the cool stone
> steps of a Baptist church and told stories to other

children. . . . We'd gather deliciously close together on the church steps and I'd "cut loose." I can remember very distinctly the smugness that came over me when one of the youngsters would run up the street calling to any stragglers, "Marjorie's going to tell stories!"[11]

Marjorie not only told stories, she also wrote them down. She began writing poetry at age six and started to dream of becoming a writer. She had a story published in the Sunday children's page of the *Washington Post* at age eleven, and at fifteen she won second place in a young authors' contest for *McCall's* magazine. Thus, before Marjorie turned sixteen, people could tell she had the makings of a writer.

College Years

Marjorie was sixteen when tragedy struck the Kinnan family. Her father became ill with a kidney infection and died on January 31, 1913. Since Marjorie was extremely close to her father, his untimely death dealt her a heavy blow. Arthur Kinnan had always planned to send his children to the University of Wisconsin, and after his death the family followed his wishes. Once Marjorie graduated from high school in the spring of 1914, Ida Kinnan moved her family to Madison, Wisconsin, where the university is located.

The following fall Marjorie enrolled as an English major. In her four years at the university she participated in many activities, including editing the school's *Literary Magazine*. It was on the staff of this magazine that she met Charles "Chuck" Rawlings. They were both editors and therefore spent a great deal of time working together. As they got to know each other, they realized they both dreamt of becoming famous writers and had a number of other things in common. Eventually, Marjorie and Charles fell in love.

While the romance between the couple blossomed, something that would keep them apart was brewing as well. Just before Marjorie entered the University of Wisconsin, World

War I had broken out in Europe. Then, in early April 1917, the United States entered the fray. Following their graduation in the spring of 1918, Charles enlisted in the armed forces, and a few months later he was ordered to report to basic training at Camp Upton on Long Island in New York. Although he and Marjorie were separated, they made a commitment to each other before Charles left—they were engaged to be married.

Taking a Bite out of the Big Apple

Fresh out of college, Marjorie was determined to make her dreams of being a writer a reality. She decided the best course of action was to try to get her foot in the door of the publishing world, and to accomplish this she moved to its center, New York City. In New York, Marjorie tried to get an entry-level position at one of the larger publishing companies, but all the jobs she was offered did not pay well, and especially did not pay women well. In the end, she accepted an editorial position with the National Board of the YWCA.

While working for this organization, Marjorie also tried to make a name for herself as a fiction writer. She found time to write and also sent out many of the stories and poems she had written in college. However, she did not have any luck getting published and was a bit discouraged about her inability to sell her work.

It was not only Marjorie's professional life that was a bit discouraging. Her personal life was difficult as well. Although New York City was relatively close to Camp Upton, she and Charles could only see each other when he had leave from camp. The couple wrote letters to each other nearly every day, but the limited time they could spend together still strained their relationship.

In addition, both Marjorie and Charles knew that Marjorie was not an easy person to deal with. Throughout her life, Marjorie had what she referred to as her "fits," "ugliness," and "temper." Marjorie was never able to control these episodes, and as a result they affected many of her personal relationships. Those who knew her well described these incidents as "causing a commotion" or "crying and carrying on." According to Marjorie, they were times when she became enraged over insignificant things and made a fool out of herself to friends and acquaintances.

Married Life

Difficult or not, Charles Rawlings loved Marjorie Kinnan, and soon after the First World War came to an end in November 1918, he asked Ida Kinnan for permission to marry her daughter. Mrs. Kinnan was less than pleased with Marjorie's taste in future husbands, but nevertheless gave her consent for the two to be married. The happy couple was wed in May 1919, and Marjorie Kinnan's new life as Marjorie Kinnan Rawlings began.

The Rawlingses moved to Louisville, Kentucky, on the recommendation of friends and got jobs with the Louisville *Courier-Journal* in 1920. Marjorie Kinnan Rawlings was a feature writer, and her husband worked as a reporter. In their free time, the couple participated in an illegal form of entertainment that would later cause problems for Marjorie—drinking. In January 1919, Congress outlawed the manufacture, sale, and transportation of alcohol in the United States. In other words, drinking was illegal, and it remained so until 1933. This nearly fourteen-year period is commonly referred to as the Prohibition era. Throughout this era, alcohol was still produced, sold, and consumed illegally, and in Louisville, Marjorie and Charles consumed a good deal of it. They drank heavily, and Rawlings enjoyed it all the more because she was defying the law.

The couple's stay in Louisville, however, was a short one. After two years of living there, writing for the *Courier-Journal,* and having no success publishing her short stories, it became apparent to Rawlings that her career was not going anywhere. Since Charles's was not either, the couple moved to Rochester, New York, in 1922.

Soon after her move to New York, Marjorie Kinnan Rawlings's life was marred by tragedy again when Ida Kinnan died in 1923. From her mother's estate, Rawlings received a small inheritance that she and Charles saved as a nest egg. Little did they know at the time, this money would later allow them to purchase the land of their dreams.

For the time being, however, Rawlings wrote feature articles for two of Rochester's local papers and also for a magazine called *5 O'clock*. Then, in 1926, she began writing a syndicated column called "Songs of a Housewife." It was quite successful, but even though Rawlings achieved some notoriety as its author, she was still unhappy with her professional writing career. It was fiction that Rawlings dreamt of writing. She had been trying to make her mark in it for nearly eight years now but had not been able to sell a single story. As a result, she was becoming disheartened.

Cross Creek

To make matters worse, Charles and Marjorie Rawlings were not getting along. In an effort to spend some time together, they took a trip to see Charles's brothers who lived in the north central interior of Florida. At the time, this portion of Florida was relatively undeveloped, and the Rawlingses fell in love with the scenic wilderness. They decided to use the money Marjorie inherited from her mother's estate to purchase an orange grove in the area known as Cross Creek. Things moved quickly, and by November they were living and working on an orange grove in Florida.

Rawlings adored Cross Creek. The uncharted wilderness seemed adventurous, and she felt immediately at home. However, she had agreed to move to Cross Creek for other reasons as well. She later wrote to her friend Bee that she had "hoped that maybe the new and exciting environment, [Charles's] two brothers being with [them] and so on, would make things all right" between her and her husband. She added that, instead, "they got steadily worse."[12]

Things grew steadily worse for the United States as well. In 1929 the stock market crashed and marked the beginning of the Great Depression. Many U.S. citizens who had enjoyed unprecedented wealth in the 1920s were forced into times of severe poverty. Luckily, the Rawlingses were not greatly affected on their orange grove, although working the grove did prove to be more demanding than they had anticipated.

Inspiration and Publication

When Rawlings moved to Cross Creek in 1928, it had been ten years since she had graduated from college and set out to make her mark on the world. She had achieved some success as the "Songs of a Housewife" columnist but still had not been recognized for the type of writing for which she most wanted to be—fiction. For nearly a decade she had sent out her stories to various magazines around the nation only to receive rejection letters in return, but all that was about to change.

Rawlings's new surroundings would come to play a very important role in her writing career. One of her biographers and critics, Gordon E. Bigelow, even claims "she needed the specific stimulus" of the Cross Creek experience to "spark her imagination," and adds that "only the Florida years [of her life] seemed to be viable artistically."[13]

The beauty of the Cross Creek area, as well as the people who lived in it, inspired Rawlings. She began taking notes, learning the names of the different types of vegetation, and watching the habits of the local people, who were called "crackers." At the time, the word *cracker* did not have the negative connotations it does today. Instead, it was used in Georgia and Florida to refer to rural white natives of English or Scottish descent. Rawlings was fascinated by these people, their personalities, their speech patterns, and the way that they lived. She carefully observed them and began to write about them.

In 1930, a little over a year after moving to Cross Creek, Rawlings sent *Scribner's Magazine* some character sketches of her new friends and neighbors. *Scribner's* wanted to publish them and offered Rawlings $150. Later that same year, she also sold *Scribner's* a novella about the trials and tribulations of a young "cracker" couple called "Jacob's Ladder." When, after more than a decade of rejection, Rawlings's sketches were printed in the February 1931 issue of *Scribner's* under the title "Cracker Chidlings," she was finally a published fiction writer.

Rawlings's publication in *Scribner's* marked the beginning of the rest of her career. This was not because "Cracker Chidlings" or "Jacob's Ladder" gained her instant notoriety. Rather, it was the fact that working with *Scribner's* brought her to the attention of Max Perkins. At the time, Perkins was the chief editor of *Scribner's*, but today he is recognized as one of the preeminent editors in the history of American literature. From 1920 until his death in 1947, he worked as an editor and confidant of Ernest Hemingway, F. Scott Fitzgerald, Thomas Wolfe, and Rawlings, among others.

Perkins recognized Rawlings's talent immediately. After the revisions of "Jacob's Ladder" were complete in early 1931, he wrote her a short letter that ended with, "Is there any chance that you will write a novel? If you do, you can depend upon a very eager and prompt consideration of it from us."[14] Rawlings immediately replied that she had four novels in mind.

South Moon Under

A little encouragement from Perkins was just the shove that Rawlings needed. With Charles's blessing, she moved in with a "cracker" family for a couple of months in 1931 and began extensive research for her first novel. Rawlings boarded with Leonard Fiddia and his mother, Piety, who lived in Big Scrub country—an area that would become the setting for many of Rawlings's novels, including *The Yearling*. The Big Scrub was a densely forested area that began about twenty-five miles away from Rawlings's home. This tract of forestland was broken up by the occasional small pond and sandwiched between the Oklawaha and St. Johns rivers. Today this area is a national forest, but in 1931 families such as the Fiddias eked out a living in it. Rawlings returned home after a few months in the scrub with extensive notes about the land and the lifestyle of those who lived on it. Quickly, she began work on her first book, *South Moon Under*.

Perkins served as her mentor and guide. She would write drafts and send them off to Perkins, and he would reply with gentle suggestions about how the book should be changed. Their hard work paid off when *South Moon Under* was published in March 1933 and reviewers praised the book, calling it "both a living document and a book of which one must say that it is distinguished art."[15] Another critic referred to it as a "deftly handled piece of fiction."[16] It was a Book-of-the-Month Club selection, and by April it was listed as the third best-seller in the *New York Herald Tribune*.

Unfortunately, the good came with the bad for Rawlings. Around the same time her book was published, she and Charles had a "showdown." According to Rawlings, they argued and Charles admitted he "had always had an inferiority complex"[17] about her literary success. The couple separated, and in November the divorce was final. In a letter to Perkins, Rawlings called this "the end, simply . . . of fourteen years of Hell."[18]

Golden Apples

Another event occurred in 1933 that seemed insignificant at the time, but later proved to be monumental. In early June, Perkins wrote to Rawlings that he wished to speak with her about possibly writing a children's book about the Florida scrub. This suggestion would evolve over time and five years later be published as her most successful novel, *The Yearling*.

However, Rawlings did not immediately begin work on *The Yearling* and decided instead to write a second adult novel first. This book, *Golden Apples,* was published in the fall of 1935 and told the story of an Englishman sent to Florida in disgrace who finds Florida scrub intolerable and marries a local scrub girl in a moment of desperation and loneliness.

Reviews of Rawlings's second book were mixed. Overall, most critics appreciated the book but pointed to various flaws such as a few points where the book seemed contrived. Percy Hutchison noted the novel lacked unity and added that "Rawlings seems unable to draw her many threads together and make a finished ending."[19]

Not surprisingly, Rawlings herself was not altogether pleased with the final manuscript, telling Perkins that she could do better and they both knew it. The book did fairly well commercially, but both Perkins and Rawlings were dissatisfied with sales. Yet they did not dwell on this disappointment, and Rawlings set to work on her next project—the children's book set in the Florida scrub.

The Yearling's Success Brings New Challenges

In the end, this children's book was Rawlings's most successful work of fiction. It took her roughly two years to complete, but was well worth the effort. When it was published in 1938 as *The Yearling*, it rocketed to the top of the best-seller lists and was unanimously praised by critics. Some even ventured to guess that one day it might be considered a classic alongside *Huckleberry Finn*, *The Jungle Book*, and various other works that appealed to both adults and youth.

The popularity of *The Yearling* made Rawlings an instant national celebrity. Now forty-two years old, the little girl who had grown up dreaming of fame and fortune as a writer had achieved it. However, her newfound fame was just one of many factors—both good and bad—that would make the remaining years of her life increasingly chaotic.

Fame brought with it new demands on Rawlings's time. Cross Creek was no longer the quiet, isolated place it used to be. Now, a variety of somewhat important people wanted to meet the famous author of *The Yearling* and see the wilderness in which it was set. Always a good hostess, Rawlings was more than happy to oblige. She received numerous dinner guests and also agreed to speaking engagements, tours, and other appearances. As a result of this busy schedule, she had less time to write.

Another factor that began to influence Rawlings's writing was her drinking. In a section of her book called "Whiskey, the Constant Companion," Idella Parker, Rawlings's maid, explained the slow progression of Rawlings's drinking from bad to worse:

> It was some time before I noticed that Mrs. Rawlings was drinking more than was good for her. . . .When it started, I can't say exactly, but I began to notice that she was also placing a bottle of whiskey, wrapped in a paper bag, right alongside the typewriter. . . . Many days I could tell when I brought lunch that she was about as [drunk] as she wanted to be, and most days after lunch she would lie down to sleep.[20]

Though Rawlings's drinking remained somewhat manageable in the years immediately following the publication of *The Yearling,* slowly it became a significant problem. Not only did it decrease the number of productive hours she could write in a day, it also caused her health problems, exacerbated her mood swings, and made it more difficult for her friends and loved ones to deal with her.

The Next Step

Norton Baskin, however, could deal with Rawlings. Baskin managed a hotel in nearby Ocala, Florida, and in the two years prior to the publication of *The Yearling* he and Rawlings became good friends. Soon after *The Yearling* was published in 1938, they began a courtship. Although Baskin was a very positive aspect of Rawlings's life, the budding relationship placed further demands on her already limited time.

Still, Rawlings was quite productive. In the spring of 1940, she published a collection of previously written short stories titled *When the Whippoorwill.* Critics loved the book, and Rawlings set to work on her next one, *Cross Creek,* a collection of autobiographical sketches about her life at the creek.

This life at the creek changed significantly in October 1941, when she married Norton Baskin. When they initially began to seriously consider marriage, Rawlings was "torn at the thought of giving up the Creek way of life."[21] Baskin had to be in Ocala to manage his hotel, and it was quite a distance from Cross Creek. Soon after their wedding, the Baskins purchased their own hotel in St. Augustine, Castle Warden, for Norton to run, but it had the same drawback that the hotel in Ocala did—it was away from Cross Creek.

Rawlings, pictured here in the garden at her beloved Cross Creek, received great acclaim with the publication of The Yearling.

From then on, Rawlings split her time between her new home— a penthouse apartment at Castle Warden—and the creek. This too became a factor that affected her writing. Idella Parker recalled that "slowly, the trips to Cross Creek became fewer and farther between, until . . . we were living almost all the time at St. Augustine. . . . When we did go back . . . the house seemed different, empty and undressed somehow."[22] According to Parker, this change was very difficult for Rawlings since the creek was where she loved to work. In St. Augustine—or even split between the two places—she was restless and had difficulty writing.

War at Home and Away

Norton Baskin unknowingly chose an inauspicious day to open his new hotel—December 7, 1941. That very same day, the Japanese bombed Pearl Harbor, and the United States entered World War II shortly thereafter. For the next few years, Rawlings had difficulty writing because two separate wars took up a great deal of her time. World War II was one; the other was a court case she became embroiled in because of her autobiography, *Cross Creek*.

In February 1942 Rawlings's autobiography was published, and critics heralded it as "deeply honest and engaging."[23] Although reviewers loved the book, one of Rawlings's Cross Creek neighbors, Zelma Cason, who was mentioned by name in *Cross Creek,* did not. In January 1943 Cason initiated a lawsuit for libel against Rawlings, claiming that passages in *Cross Creek* embarrassed her and caused her pain.

A few months later, World War II began to play a more significant role in Rawlings's daily life when Norton Baskin—despite his age of forty-one—enlisted as an ambulance driver in the American Field Service. A heartbroken Rawlings researched and found out that "these outfits worked in the front lines and that in the last war their casualties were twice the ratio of regular army casualties."[24] Baskin left and Rawlings worried about him every day he was away.

She filled her days by doing her part to help the war effort. Rawlings wrote publicity items for the National War Front as well as many letters to individual servicemen. Then, in 1944, she received word that Baskin was very ill and pulled every string she could to get him safely home. It worked, and he returned in the late fall of 1944—although still quite sick. Luckily, by the time World War II came to a close in the fall of 1945, Baskin had recovered and was back running his hotel.

Although the war ended in 1945, Rawlings's legal one was just beginning. Cason's lawsuit—typically referred to as the Cross Creek trial—went to trial in 1946. The charges had been changed to invasion of privacy and Cason's lawyers contended that she "had lived a quiet life until Marjorie Rawlings had maliciously brought on her undesirable and obnoxious publicity."[25] Rawlings's lawyers argued that the author simply wrote the truth about a woman who was her friend. In the end, Rawlings was found not guilty by the jury, but the trial was not finished. Cason's lawyers appealed to the Florida State Supreme Court, and in 1947 the court's final verdict was handed down. Rawlings had to pay Cason $1 plus reimburse her legal fees.

The Sojourner

Thus, in the end, the trial was merely a time-consuming and somewhat expensive annoyance for Rawlings. However, for nearly five years she focused her attention on this trial, as well as World War II and Baskin's recovery. Although all these things were very important to her, they left little time for writing. As a result, even though Rawlings had written to Perkins in 1945 telling him she was set to begin work on her next novel, *The Sojourner,* she had completed very little of the manuscript by the summer of 1947.

Then, on June 17, 1947, Max Perkins, Rawlings's mentor and guide, died. Rawlings later wrote she felt an unspeakable grief when she heard the news. Idella Parker recalled the profound effect it had on Rawlings:

> His death shocked her very much, and she just could not seem to get over it. She would walk through the house, wringing her hands and crying. . . . She would . . . walk the floors for hours, smoking and drinking, calling out his name. She could not seem to settle down to her work, and her writing just fell off.[26]

After Perkins's death, the writing of *The Sojourner* became even more difficult. All of the factors that kept Rawlings from writing seemed to combine: She was drinking more heavily; she was away from Cross Creek a great deal; and now the man who had provided support and guidance for her work was dead. In 1949, she started on the manuscript again; however, it was slow going and things got in the way. For starters, Rawlings felt depressed and was possibly even suicidal. Also, her drinking had reached a point where even Rawlings realized it was affecting her writing. As a result, there were a few times in the 1950s that she tried to stop drinking and went for a few days, even weeks, without alcohol. During these periods she found that her writing improved, but a week later she would be drinking again.

In the fall of 1950 Rawlings finished the first draft of *The Sojourner*. The revision process went slowly and was further delayed when Rawlings was treated for a coronary spasm in February 1952. The book was finally published in January 1953 and was a departure for Rawlings—it was not set in the Florida scrub as her previous novels were. Instead, the story took place on a farm west of the Hudson River Valley and told the tale of two brothers. The critics agreed it was a "good book," but some thought that it seemed to "lack excitement and fire"[27] that her earlier works had.

Rawlings next set to work on a biography of Pulitzer Prize–winning author Ellen Glasgow, but it would never be completed. On December 12, 1953, she had a brain hemorrhage—a blood vessel in her brain burst. Doctors told Norton Baskin that Rawlings was alive and if no other blood vessels burst, she could live a normal life, but that was not to be. On December 14, 1953, another blood vessel burst and Marjorie Kinnan Rawlings Baskin died.

Rawlings's will named a friend, Julia Scribner, as her literary executor, and following her death Scribner oversaw the posthumous publication of two of Rawlings's works. In 1955, *The Secret River* was published. It was a children's book that told the story of an African American child named Calpurnia. The book received the Newbery Medal of Honor in 1956, but, as is the case with many children's books, very little critical attention was paid to it. The other publication was *The Marjorie Kinnan Rawlings Reader*, a collection of short stories and excerpts from her novels. However, even with these two new books added to her body of work, it is still the ever-popular *The Yearling* for which Rawlings is remembered.

CHAPTER TWO

The History of *The Yearling*

Samuel I. Bellman points out that "the enormous popular success of *The Yearling*" is now "a commonplace of twentieth-century publishing history in this country."[28] Terms such as *American classic* or *timeless classic* are easily attached to descriptions of the novel. Each year—now more than half a century after its initial publication—thousands of people purchase *The Yearling,* and it is a staple in the curriculum of various schools across the United States. Moreover, the history of this popular novel is nearly as exciting as the book itself.

Indecision

The wheels were set in motion on June 1, 1933. It was on this fateful day that Max Perkins wrote a short letter to Marjorie Kinnan Rawlings. He briefly replied to some questions she had, and closed by saying he wished to discuss a plan he had for her "in connection with writing." Rawlings's interest was piqued, and eventually she coaxed him into explaining his plan. He wrote,

> I was simply going to suggest that you do a book about
> a child in the scrub, which would be designed for what
> we have to call younger readers. . . . If you wrote about
> a child's life, whether a girl or a boy, or both, it would

certainly be a fine publication. . . . Such a book would require very little plot. Its interest would simply be that of character and that of the peculiar & adventurous life.[29]

This suggestion eventually led to Rawlings's most successful book, but she originally reacted with "sheer distress." It appears she was somewhat insulted by being asked to write a children's book, but at the same time the idea intrigued her.

By the middle of June 1933 Rawlings had a general idea that she would write an adventure book for young readers set in the Florida scrub. However, the actual writing of the novel was still years away because a great many things had to be resolved before she could begin. Chief among these was what to write first, her second adult novel or the "boy's book," as she and Perkins called it.

Rawlings changed her mind time and again, so the research for the two books went on simultaneously. Originally, she decided to first write the adult book—later titled *Golden Apples*—and embarked on an extended trip to England to gather material about her main character, an Englishman transplanted in the Florida scrub. But when she returned home, she was in what she called a "distressed mental condition." Rawlings believed the writing of the complex Englishman might be too much for her in her condition and toyed with the idea of first writing the "boy's book," believing it would be uncomplicated and easier to write.

In an effort to gather background information for this book, Rawlings went to stay with Cal Long and his wife, who had lived in the heart of the scrub land since 1872. Long and another old hunter named Barney Dillard supplied the majority of Rawlings's background information about the way people lived in the scrub and its history for *The Yearling*. She went to stay with Long for a week in early October to gather material and came back to Cross Creek with plans to return to the Longs' home in the near future.

Although she seemed genuinely excited about writing the book upon her return, about a week later Rawlings fired off a long letter to Perkins that implied that she found the idea of writing a book for young readers insulting. The letter stated that she would write the book only if it were "an out-and-out juvenile [book]" because she did not want any "pretense at an adult book."[30] Later on in the same letter, she requested that the book not be published under her name, or at least not her full name. She said this was because she feared that boys would not read an adventure book written by a woman, but the general tone of the letter suggests that this request was for other reasons such as anger or embarrassment.

Another letter that she wrote to Perkins in November provides some insight into the factors that may have caused Rawlings's hostility that October day. It turns out the angry letter was written a few weeks before her divorce from Charles Rawlings became final. According to Rawlings, in the weeks before their divorce, Charles tried to convince her that Perkins was suggesting the boy's book because he knew the novel she wished to write, *Golden Apples*, would be a failure. Although Perkins could not have known the source of her dismay at the time, he quickly replied to her October letter. He immediately understood the problem—Rawlings was worried he had no faith in her ability to write a serious adult novel—and carefully massaged her bruised ego. He replied,

> I am thinking of a book about a boy, but his age is not important. Every boy between twelve and eighteen who lives an outdoor life is interested in the same things. In a general way . . . I associate with it such books as "Huckleberry Finn," Kipling's "Kim," David Crockett's Memoirs, "Treasure Island," and "The Hoosier School Boy." All these books are primarily *for boys*. All of them are read by men, and they are the favorite books of some men. The truth is the best part of a man is a boy.[31]

Rawlings felt much better when she realized she was expected not just to write a juvenile book but a boys' classic on the level of Mark Twain's *Adventures of Huckleberry Finn*.

A Feeling to Capture and a Story to Tell

In the end Rawlings decided to write *Golden Apples* before the boy's book, but as she wrote, the material she had gathered from Cal Long incubated in the back of her mind. *Golden Apples* was published in the fall of 1935. Soon after, Rawlings wrote to Perkins telling him she just did not "have the enthusiasm"[32] for writing the book for younger readers. It had been two years since her stay with Long and now she felt her material was insufficient. Perhaps even more disconcerting was the fact that she had no idea what she wanted the story to be about or what she wanted to say with the book.

The future of the boy's book looked bleak, but a few weeks later Perkins received a more encouraging letter. Rawlings had figured out what she wanted to do with the book. "It will not be a story for boys, though some of them might enjoy it," she wrote. "It will be a story *about* a boy—a brief and tragic idyll [a charming, simple tale] of boyhood."[33]

Rawlings had decided to convey a feeling similar to one she had when she was sixteen. It was a beautiful April day—like those at the beginning and end of *The Yearling*—after her father died and she had a "premonition of maturity." In a radio talk for a Voice of America series Rawlings described her feelings on that April day:

> I remember the delirious excitement I felt [about the day being so beautiful]. And at the height of my delight, a sadness came over me, and I understood suddenly that I should not always be a child, and that beyond this carefree moment life was waiting with its responsibilities.[34]

The Yearling was inspired by this day and the mixed emotions Rawlings felt about life and responsibility at that moment. Perhaps for this reason, Jody Baxter exhibits some of these same emotions on his April day, the last day that *The Yearling* covers. Flag is dead and Jody is returning home after running away to the river when he realizes that it is April.

> A memory stirred him. He had come here [to the creek] a year ago, on a bland and tender day. He had splashed in the creek water and lain, as now, among the ferns and grasses. Something had been fine and lovely. He had built himself a flutter-mill. He rose and moved with a quickening of his pulse to the location. It seemed to him that if he found it, he would discover with it all the other things that had vanished. The flutter-mill was gone. The flood had washed it away, and all its merry turning.
>
> He thought stubbornly, "I'll build me another."
>
> He [built it]. . . . But it was only palmetto strips brushing the water. There was no magic in the motion. The flutter-mill had lost its comfort. . . .
>
> He kicked it apart with one foot. . . . He threw himself on the ground and sobbed bitterly. There was no comfort anywhere.[35]

Thus, as was the case with Rawlings on her April day, Jody too knows that he cannot forever remain a carefree child.

While the emotions Rawlings was trying to convey were her own, the story of the pet deer was one she had heard from Long. There is some discrepancy between the various biographical accounts of her life as to whether it was Cal or his brother Mel who actually had a pet fawn as a child. Either way, Rawlings learned the story of the fawn's growth, the way it acted in the home, and the reason it had to be shot, from Long. Armed with this story and her overarching desire to convey the agony of the end of childhood, Rawlings set to work on *The Yearling*.

The Setting

Rawlings used an area known as Pat's Island as the setting for her novel. In his book *Frontier Eden*, Gordon E. Bigelow states that *The Yearling* country is "centered on a pine island known in real life as Pat's Island—the Baxter's Island of the book—located about two miles west of Silver Glen Springs which rises near the shore of Lake George."[36] According to Bigelow, other locations that are described in the book such as Juniper Springs, Fort Gates, and Volusia all lie within a ten-mile radius of this patch of pine trees surrounded by scrub land.

The story takes place from 1870–1871, roughly five years after the end of the Civil War, at a time when Florida was still a frontier state. The fact that *The Yearling* characters Penny and Easy Ozell both fought in the Civil War—although on different sides—is mentioned in passing. The time period is also evident when Penny and Jody trade Mr. Boyles venison that he sells to the tourist boats going down the St. Johns. Here, Rawlings is utilizing the fact that, in 1870, Jacksonville—which was devastated by the war—began to bounce back and became a tourist attraction. According to historian Michael Gannon, it was considered "the gateway to southern Florida via the St. Johns River."[37] Various steamer companies carried Northerners and Southerners alike down the St. Johns, and new hotels sprang up along the way to accommodate travelers.

Finally, the book contains an account of a terrible storm that causes it to rain for more than a week and devastates much of the scrub. This is based on an actual storm that occurred in 1871. Thus, Rawlings uses small clues such as the storm, the presence of Civil War veterans, and the tourist activity on the river to indicate the year in which the novel takes place, but she never actually mentions it. This is most likely because the era is used merely as a backdrop for the story and has little relevance to the actual plot. The reader gets the impression that the story could take place at any time when unsettled, wilderness conditions existed in the United States.

Writing

Having settled on a time and place for the story, Rawlings set about working on *The Yearling*. Though she did not get much work done on the book in the winter of 1935—Rawlings argued that it was nearly impossible for her to write in the winter—by July she informed Perkins that she had pretty much all the priceless material she needed for the book and just had to sit down and write it out. She had gotten more material through visiting with an old pioneer named Barney Dillard who lived on the St. Johns River and took her hunting.

However, her writing did not go well, and finally Rawlings decided there was only one way to get the job done. "I simply could not get going on the book [at the creek]," she wrote to Perkins. "Things were on my nerves—mosquitoes bad, heat sticky and depressing, grove responsibilities wearing. . . . [I] Decided just to bolt for the mountains."[38] In September 1936, Rawlings rented a cottage in the mountains of North Carolina in a town called Banner Elk. Her relocation was an attempt to jump-start the book, and it worked. The book began to move slowly but steadily ahead.

When she returned to Cross Creek a month later, Rawlings once again struggled with writing. Visitors and the orange grove demanded her time. Frustrated by this, she joked with Perkins that she was likely to explode. Rawlings finally sent Perkins a rough draft in June 1937 and then drove up to New York to see friends and meet with him. Perkins apparently had some useful criticism of her draft when she saw him, because she later wrote from her hotel on Long Island, "Why didn't you tell me how *sappy* 'The Yearling' was? It has a saccharine stupidity of style and movement."[39]

Rawlings returned home to rewrite and revise her manuscript. In December, she sent Perkins her first draft, and he promptly replied that he read the book with "the very greatest pleasure" and "constantly growing interest."[40] Perkins suggested a few revisions: the Forresters be made tougher; an "unseemly performance" of Ma Forrester be cut out of the book (apparently it was); and the whole work be tightened overall. However, for the most part the novel was complete—and good.

Important Similarities and Differences

The Yearling was a good book for numerous reasons. For starters, its foundation was Rawlings's expert use of the native dialect and beautiful descriptions of nature that were also the strength of her earlier novels. However, in *The Yearling* Rawlings was also able to avoid some of the pitfalls that plagued *South Moon Under* and *Golden Apples*. According to critic Gordon E. Bigelow, one of the most significant shortcomings of her earlier books was her inability to strike a balance between the use of fact and fiction. Her goal in previous works had been to explain the Florida scrub region and the way people lived within it; the characters in these books were insignificant. Bigelow writes that, as a result, they were "much more typical crackers than they [were] unique human beings."[41]

The same cannot be said for Jody and Penny Baxter. Although both speak in the dialect of the Florida natives and live life in the scrub, they are people first and "crackers" second. Early reviews of *The Yearling* clearly attest to this. In her *New York Times Book Review*, Edith H. Walton wrote that Rawlings had been able to convey the dialect and habits of "crackers" in her previous works, but "never before, however, has she created a set of characters who are so close and real to the reader."[42] William Soskin was particularly impressed by Jody. He raved,

Jody, roaming in the scrub forests of Mrs. Rawlings' favorite Florida country, living close to his animals with

a sensitive understanding of them, learning the subtleties of life which a child in sophisticated communities can never know, and reflecting that wholesomeness
in his own spirit, has a gayety and a bubbling humor
which run far deeper than that of any of the famous
adolescents of our literature.[43]

However, it was not merely the characters that made *The
Yearling* Rawlings's finest work. Another key, according to
Bigelow, is the structure that she chose for the book. Although
the overarching story is Jody's passage from childhood to maturity, the book is actually made up of numerous anecdotes: bear
hunts, trips to Volusia, his friend Fodder-wing's death, fights,
Flag's antics, and many more. Bigelow writes, "Marjorie's narrative talent was chiefly that of raconteur, a teller of tales, and
she always shows best in the short haul in particular scenes and
anecdotes."[44] Thus, the structure she chose for the book
allowed her to write it as numerous short anecdotes, and therefore her best talents as a storyteller emerged.

Publication and Reaction

In February 1938, five years after it was first mentioned, the
children's book about the scrub was published. It was a
regional novel at a time when regional literature was enjoying a great deal of popularity in the United States. The book
received rave reviews. The *New York Times* declared that
"despite her previous accomplishments, Mrs. Rawlings has
written nothing even comparable in excellence to 'The
Yearling.'"[45] *Time* magazine even predicted, "with its excellent descriptions of Florida scrub landscapes, its skillful use
of native vernacular, its tender relation between Jody and his
pet fawn, *The Yearling* is a simply written, picturesque story
of boyhood that stands a good chance, when adults have finished with it, of finding a permanent place in adolescent
libraries."[46]

This scene from the movie vividly brings to life the character of Jody and his love for the orphaned fawn.

The Yearling enjoyed immediate commercial success. It was a Book-of-the-Month Club selection, and in a matter of weeks stood atop the best-seller lists, selling 265,000 copies in 1938 alone. It went on to become the number-one selling book that year and remained popular enough throughout 1939 to secure a spot as the seventh best-seller. The movie rights were quickly snatched up by Metro Goldwyn Mayer for $30,000. And in 1939, it was awarded the Pulitzer Prize in fiction.

In the years since its initial publication, *The Yearling* has become just what some early critics believed it would—an American classic. In some ways the book is anchored in time and confronts some of the same problems that other classics, such as *Adventures of Huckleberry Finn* and *Tom Sawyer*, do. Most notably, at times, *The Yearling* has been pulled from the shelves of some school libraries because of allegations of racism, a racism that was sadly commonplace when Rawlings wrote the novel. Today, the editions of the novel that are published have been edited and different terms are used to describe African Americans, thereby eliminating the book's original racist language.

However, like its counterparts, there is also something timeless about *The Yearling*. It masterfully communicates the emotions of the "death" of childhood, a testament to the fact that Rawlings captured on paper that April day she set out to portray. Although the challenges and disappointments of growth from childhood to young adulthood have changed, the emotions experienced have not. *The Yearling* still appeals to some young readers today, and it seems it will continue to do so in years to come.

CHAPTER THREE

The Plot

The *Yearling* tells of Jody Baxter's passage from boyhood to maturity in the Florida scrub. It covers one year, beginning in April 1870 when he is twelve and ending the following April. Over the course of this year, events in Jody's life teach him about death, starvation, loyalty, love, and the responsibilities he must accept to become an adult.

The book begins on a beautiful April day on the Baxter farm, a hundred-acre tract of land they call Baxter's Island, not because it is surrounded by water but because it is a cluster of long-leaf pines amid a sea of scrub land. The only drawback to the property is the scarcity of water. Rawlings informs readers that "water for the inhabitants of Baxter's Island must come . . . from the great sink-hole on the [farm's] western boundary."[47] The only human inhabitants of Baxter's Island are Jody Baxter, his mother Ora "Ma" Baxter, and his father Ezra "Penny" Baxter.

As the book opens, twelve-year-old Jody Baxter is in the fields hoeing corn. But giving in to his desire to play, Jody soon abandons his work and responsibilities. As he wanders miles to the bank of a spring, he longs for a pet. The Baxters do have three dogs—old Julia, Rip, and Perk—but these animals are Penny's loyal work dogs. The reader learns that Jody "would like anything that was his own; that licked his face and followed him as old Julia followed his father."[48]

When he reaches the spring, Jody constructs a "flutter mill," a water wheel made from twigs and palm leaves. He watches his creation turn until he falls asleep—lazing the day away and completely neglecting his chores. That evening when Jody returns home, he discovers that his father is not mad at him for running off to play. In fact, he covered for Jody. "I never let on you wasn't here," Penny tells his son. "She [Ma Baxter] said, 'where's Jody?' and I said, 'Oh, I reckon he's around some'eres.'"[49]

Hunting Old Slewfoot

The next morning Jody and Penny awake to find the partially eaten carcass of their sow. Jody examines the tracks alongside the sow's carcass and knows instantly what killed her—Old Slewfoot, a giant bear with one toe missing on his right front paw. Old Slewfoot has troubled the Baxters for years and now he has killed the sow but taken only one bite of her meat. "That's why I hate a bear," Penny tells Jody. "A creetur that kills and eats what he needs, why, he's jest like the rest of us, makin' out the best he kin. But an animal, or a person either, that'll do harm jest to be a-doin'—You look in a bear's face and you'll see he's got no remorse."[50]

After breakfast, Jody and Penny go on a hunt for Old Slewfoot. Jody enjoys hunting with his father and the Baxter dogs. Penny is a great hunter, famous in the region for his ability to find game, and Jody marvels at his knowledge and understanding of animal behavior. As they hunt, Penny explains an important part of his ideology to his son. He warns Jody, "Don't you grow up like the Forresters, killin' meat you got no use for, for the fun of it. That's evil as the bears."[51]

The Forresters of whom Penny speaks are the Baxters' closest neighbors. About four miles from Baxter's Island, Ma and Pa Forrester live with their seven sons—Buck, Mill-Wheel, Arch, Lem, Gabby, Pack, and Fodder-wing. With the exception of the youngest, Fodder-wing, the Forrester brothers are all large, burly, quarrelsome, and raucous men.

As Jody and his father hunt for Old Slewfoot, Penny teaches his son valuable lessons about animal behavior and about life.

Jody heeds his father's words and they continue their hunt. When the dogs catch up to Old Slewfoot, Julia and Rip pursue the bear, but the Baxters' new dog, Perk, runs away to hide. The two older dogs corner the bear and Penny tries to shoot, but his gun backfires and Old Slewfoot attacks old Julia. To save his dog, Penny runs toward the bear and jams his gun in the bear's ribs. Eventually, Old Slewfoot retreats and swims off down the creek. The hunters all head home, defeated, with Penny carrying his wounded dog. Along the way, they come across a frightened Perk, who they now know is useless as a hunting dog. Penny explains to his son that some dogs are bear-dogs and some are not. Perk is not.

A Night at the Forresters

When father and son return from the hunt, Ma helps them work to save old Julia. The next morning the dog is better, but very tired from loss of blood. Penny knows that, in order for his family to survive in the scrub, he must have a gun that works properly. He announces that he'll take Jody to the Forresters' cabin to trade Perk for one. Ma Baxter is against the idea, not only because then Jody will not be home to help her during the day but also because she dislikes the Forresters and does not want Jody to pick up any of their bad habits. Still, against Ma's wishes, Penny and Jody leave for the Forresters'.

When Penny and Jody arrive at the Forresters', Fodder-wing takes Jody to see his animal collection and lets him hold a baby raccoon. Fodder-wing is the Forresters' crippled, hunchbacked, "witless" son and a good friend of Jody's. Seeing Fodder-wing's animals, Jody longs for a pet, but knows Ma Baxter will not allow it. She is happy to feed animals that do some sort of work on the Baxter farm but cannot tolerate feeding an animal that is only a pet.

Inside the Forrester cabin, Jody watches in awe as Penny, without being dishonest, cleverly leads Lem Forrester to believe that Perk is a great bear-hunting dog. Penny then gives Perk to Lem in exchange for a beautiful new gun. Once the trade is made, Penny rides off for home, but Jody stays to spend the night and play with Fodder-wing.

In the middle of the night at the Forresters' cabin, Jody is awakened by the sound of shouting. In the living room he finds the Forrester dogs chasing an animal that has gotten into the house. After the varmint is chased out, no one can sleep, so the Forrester brothers pull out the liquor and drink and play music. Lem begins to sing about his sweetheart. When Jody asks who she is, Lem says Twink Weatherby and Jody blurts out that she's Oliver Hutto's gal. "You say that agin in your life, boy, and you'll not have a tongue left to say it with,"[52] Lem replies. Jody keeps quiet because he is afraid of Lem, but doing so makes him feel disloyal to Oliver Hutto, a young man whom Jody idolizes and considers his best friend.

Trouble in Volusia

Weeks pass before Jody's next adventure, and in the meantime he tends to his chores, even cleaning the sinkhole to keep the Baxters' water supply clean. Jody also receives a wonderful gift from his father. Penny finds a dead albino raccoon and makes a knapsack out of its hide for his son. Although the weeks are marred a bit when Jody manages to make himself sick by eating too many brierberries, his illness only lasts two days, and when he is better, he and Penny go fishing. They not only catch fish that afternoon, but also have the opportunity to see the whooping cranes dance at sunset.

When May rolls around, Jody notices that the fawns are being born and longs to have one as a pet. He begs Ma Baxter to let him tame one, but she says no as Penny listens quietly to his son's pleas. In an effort to cheer Jody up, Penny takes him hunting the next morning. The goal is to shoot a few bucks, take the meat to trade at the store, and stop and see Grandma Hutto.

Grandma Hutto is Oliver's mother and actually of no blood relation to the Baxters. She is simply a great friend of Penny's with whom Jody and Ma stayed for four years while Penny left to fight in the Civil War. Grandma Hutto lives in a nearby town where Penny grew up called Volusia, which lies on the opposite bank of St. Johns River.

Jody is excited both to see Grandma Hutto and for the hunt. While hunting he sees a doe and its fawn. Penny even gives him a chance to bring down a buck by himself, but Jody's shot is a bit high and he only wounds the deer. When Penny finishes the job and Jody sees the dead deer, he feels ill and tells Penny, "I wisht we could git our meat without killin' it."[53] Penny agrees, but adds that they have to eat in order to survive.

Father and son take the meat to Boyles's store in Volusia to trade, and there Jody sees the store owner's niece whom he has a crush on, Eulalie Boyles. Since Jody does not have the maturity to deal with girls yet, the visit ends with him throwing a potato at Eulalie and getting in trouble with his father. After this embarrassing incident, Penny and Jody go to Grandma Hutto's house. She is excited to see them, and the three spend the night laughing and talking.

The next morning, Jody is awakened at Grandma Hutto's by the sound of a steamer and soon realizes that it is Oliver coming home from the sea. Once he gets in the house, Oliver tells tales of his adventures and gives each one of them a present. Jody is excited to receive his gift, a new hunting knife, but Oliver's generosity makes him feel guilty about not standing up to Lem weeks ago at the Forresters'. Jody worries that he betrayed Oliver and eases his conscience by telling him what Lem said. Oliver is not disturbed by the news, but leaves shortly after breakfast to go see Twink Weatherby. Jody is upset by Oliver's leaving because he wanted to spend more time with his friend. He feels that Oliver has betrayed him to spend time with a girl.

Just a little while after Oliver leaves, a friend of Grandma's named Easy Ozell comes running toward her home to tell Penny and Jody that Oliver is in trouble. Easy says Oliver is fighting three Forresters—Buck, Mill-Wheel, and Lem—and losing badly. As Penny and Jody run toward Boyles's store where the fight is raging, Penny tells Jody they will fight "for whoever's takin' a lickin' and that's Oliver."[54]

Upon hearing this, Jody worries that the Baxters cannot survive in the scrub without the Forresters as friends and ponders the nature of loyalty again. He thinks perhaps Oliver deserves his punishment for leaving to go see a girl. Jody tells Penny he refuses to fight for Oliver, but when they arrive, he thinks, "three against one was never fair. Even when the dogs bayed a bear or panther it seemed to him an uneven matter."[55] Jody jumps in the fight on Oliver's side, but is quickly knocked out by a much larger, much older Lem.

Penny is proud of Jody for fighting to help a friend.

When Jody comes to, he is in Grandma Hutto's house and his head and neck hurt from the fight. Penny has a bandaged wrist and a black eye, and Oliver is alive, but badly beaten. This was Jody's first fight, and Penny says he is proud of him for fighting to help a friend. Jody remembers that the Forresters are also his friends, and when Penny says they probably will not see the Forresters anymore, Jody feels terrible. He will miss Fodder-wing.

Snakebite

In the latter part of June, the Baxters discover their hogs have disappeared. Penny worries that the Forresters trapped them to exact their revenge for Penny and Jody coming to Oliver's rescue. He sets off with Jody to find the hogs. When they spot horse tracks next to hog tracks on a trail to the Forrester farm, Penny's suspicions are confirmed. He and Jody head toward the Forrester home to retrieve their livestock.

Along the trail, a rattlesnake strikes at Penny without warning. Penny shoots the snake, but not before it bites him. Knowing the poison is deadly, when Penny sees a doe, he shoots it, splits open his arm that the snake bit, and uses the doe's organs to draw some of the poison out of the snakebite. Hurriedly, Penny gives Jody instructions. Jody must go to the Forresters and get them to ride to get Doc Wilson while Penny heads back home. Jody and Penny are both uncertain as to whether the Forresters will help them, but Jody must try.

They set out toward the road and Jody sees that the doe his father killed had a fawn. When they part company at the road, Jody runs to the Forresters'. This is a test of Jody's bravery and courage. Although he is afraid of being beaten, he must face the Forresters and ask for help for his father's sake. When he reaches the Forresters' home, Lem comes out to meet him. A frightened Jody bursts into tears, telling Lem that Penny was bitten by a snake, and when the other Forresters come out of the house Jody begs them to ride for the doctor. Mill-Wheel quickly agrees to ride to Branch for Doc Wilson, and Buck offers to ride and pick up Penny. As Jody walks home in the rain worrying about the possible death of his father, he understands for the first time what it might feel like to be alone in the world without his father to care for and protect him.

The Fawn

Jody gets home to find Buck, Mill-Wheel, Penny, Ma, and Doc Wilson all at the house. He goes to check on Penny, who is alive, but Doc Wilson is uncertain whether he will survive the poisoning. Jody keeps an all-night vigil at his father's bedside. He remembers the fawn: "The fawn was all alone in the night, as he had been alone. The catastrophe that might take his father, had made it motherless. . . . He pressed his face into the hanging covers of [Penny's] bed and cried bitterly.

He was torn with hate for all death and pity for all alone-ness."[56] Jody awakes in the morning and Penny is alive and breathing more easily. Everyone is excited he is doing well, even Buck and Mill-Wheel.

Since Penny is a bit better, the others work out some details. First, Jody gives Doc Wilson his cherished, albino rac-coon knapsack as a token of his appreciation—and payment for his services—before the doctor heads home. Then, Buck offers to stay and help on the Baxter farm, and Ma reluctant-ly accepts his offer.

Jody wants to keep the orphaned fawn. He broaches the topic with his mother, but she is unreceptive. Later, he goes in to see his father and asks if he can go get the fawn and bring it home to raise. Penny says that he can, and Jody tells his mother. When she takes a firm stand, all the men back up Jody, pointing out that since Penny killed the doe it wouldn't be right to leave the fawn to starve. Mill-Wheel heads home and Jody rides with him to find the fawn. Along the way, they make peace about the fight in Volusia and Mill-Wheel assures Jody the hogs will soon be back. Jody also finds out that Fodder-wing is ill. So Jody can visit his ailing friend, Mill-Wheel agrees to send for him when Lem is away—Lem is the only Forrester holding a grudge against the Baxters—and then leaves Jody to find the fawn.

Jody finds the young animal and takes it home. He shows Penny, who is excited. Ma, on the other hand, still disapproves, and Penny speaks sternly to her, telling her she should not complain about the fawn. Jody makes a bed for the fawn in the shed. With his new pet, Jody feels happy, comforted, and no longer lonely. He is certain that having the fawn means he will never feel alone in the world again the way he did the night before. Jody dotes on the fawn and it stays by him, watches him, and plays with him. However, it still doesn't have a name. Buck suggests that since Fodder-wing is good at naming things, Jody should allow him to name the fawn.

The Death of Fodder-wing

Buck and Jody work the Baxter farm, hunt, and even gather honey while Penny recovers. In a little while, Penny is healthy enough for Buck to return home. Soon after, Buck sends word that Lem is away and Jody can bring his fawn to show Fodder-wing.

However, when Jody reaches the Forresters', he learns that Fodder-wing succumbed to his ailments. This is Jody's first encounter with the death of someone he loves. Buck leads Jody into the cabin to see his departed friend. Fodder-wing is laid out in his room, his mother crying at his side. The sight of her grief frightens Jody, as does Fodder-wing's lifeless face. When he speaks to Fodder-wing and Fodder-wing does not reply, Jody understands that death is "a silence that gave back no answer. Fodder-wing would never speak to him again."[57]

Although they ignore his presence, Jody senses that the Forresters expect him to stay. At dinner Ma Forrester tells Jody Fodder-wing dreamt of seeing the fawn and adds that he even named it Flag. Jody decides to name the fawn Flag both because he likes the name and out of respect for his friend. After supper, Jody finally comes to understand what it is the Forresters expect from him when Pa Forrester remarks, "Hit'd pleasure him, you comin' to set up with him tonight. . . . And 'twouldn't scarcely be decent, buryin' him in the mornin' without you was here. He didn't have no friend but you."[58] In other words, the Forresters expect him to stay because it would make Fodder-wing happy to have his friend there.

Jody sits up all night with the Forresters, and in the morning Penny arrives to provide assistance in their time of need. Penny builds a coffin for Fodder-wing and agrees to lead the Forresters in a prayer service. Following the funeral, Penny and Jody head home in silence.

Flood and Plague

As time passes, Jody misses Fodder-wing and finds comfort in his relationship with Flag. Jody loves the fawn, and they do everything together. Jody even tells him all his thoughts, feelings, and dreams. Flag is growing and becoming more intelligent. The fawn can open doors and starts getting into things.

In early September, a torrential rain storm causes severe flooding and threatens to destroy the Baxters' food supply. Luckily, they are able to salvage some of the crops through hard work and Penny's quick thinking. The rain stops after eight days, and soon after Buck and Mill-Wheel come to check on the Baxters. They go with Penny and Jody to ascertain the extent of the damage to the scrub and surrounding areas. The group sees the rotting carcasses of dead animals out in plain sight.

When October rolls around, Penny realizes that something is still wrong in the scrub because the smell of death lingers. He and Jody investigate and find heaps of deer carcasses. Penny concludes that the deer died from a plague he calls "the black tongue," and fears he will not be able to provide for his family if the game animals continue to perish. Jody, on the other hand, worries about Flag and wonders if he will die from the plague.

Wolf Trouble

By November, Penny and the Forresters can estimate the plague's effect on their winter food supply. Flag, however, begins to further threaten the Baxters' reserves. He ruins some sweet potatoes, and the Baxters are left with barely enough for the year. Since Flag's antics are beginning to pose a threat to the Baxters' meager food supply, Penny is angry and insists that Flag be penned when Jody cannot watch him. Jody tries to pen Flag, but Flag quickly jumps out of the enclosure. Fortunately, the potatoes are cured and there is nothing left for the fawn to bother.

Toward the end of the month, the predatory animals that did not die during the flood and the plague are starving. One evening a pack of hungry wolves kills the Baxters' heifer-calf. Penny knows the three Baxters cannot defend themselves against a pack of starving wolves and enlists the aid of the Forresters. The Forresters decide to poison the wolves, and although Penny argues that poisoning is not fair to the animals, they do it anyway. The poison kills thirty wolves in one week, leaving about a dozen on the prowl.

The Forrester brothers, Penny, and Jody go in search of the remaining pack of wolves. When they find the pack, Lem also sees a beautiful buck nearby, but does not shoot it because it will alert the wolves to their presence. At that point, killing the wolves is more important than bringing down the deer.

The Baxters are dismayed to find that one of their calves has been killed by ravenous wolves.

The Forresters, Penny, and Jody hunt and kill the remaining wolves and also capture ten live bear cubs the wolves had treed. They decide the Forresters should take the cubs to the coast and sell them. Penny asks them to stop at his home before they leave and get a list of items he wants in exchange for his share of the cubs. When they part ways, Lem suspects that Penny is really going to hunt the buck they saw earlier. Lem believes the buck belongs to him since he passed up the shot earlier in order to get the wolves. Penny assures him he will not hunt the buck.

After leaving the Forresters, Penny and Jody set out to hunt an alligator for the dogs to eat and soon have one. On their way home they come across a large buck protecting its doe. Penny shoots it, and they take it back to the Baxter home. When the Forresters stop the next morning to get Penny's list, Lem spots the buck's hide stretched out on the smokehouse wall. He is certain Penny hunted the buck he promised he would not. Lem wants to fight, but Penny calmly tells Buck the truth—that he got the deer purely by chance—and Buck calms Lem down. Through this incident, Jody learns an important lesson about how to keep a cool head and resolve differences without fighting. Buck assures Penny that he will get his even portion of the cub bounty. When the Forresters return from the coast in December, Buck is true to his word. However, the quarrel between Penny and Lem leaves relations between the families strained.

Old Slewfoot Comes for Christmas

In the latter part of December, the Baxters decide they will spend Christmas with Grandma Hutto in Volusia and join the potluck celebration at the church. Penny shoots deer to trade at Boyles's store for food, gifts, and some new material for his wife's new Christmas dress. Ma sews her new frock and the Baxters make preparations for their trip.

Then, four days before Christmas, Buck stops to tell Penny that Old Slewfoot visited the Forrester farm and to be on the lookout. That night Penny sets a trap and stays up with the dogs to watch for the bear. Still, in the morning, Penny's calf is gone. Penny tells Ma and Jody, "I've had a bait of it. . . . I mean to track that creetur down if I foller him clare to Jacksonville. This time, hit's me or him."[59] Jody is allowed to go along, but his father warns him that the pace will be fast and he does not want any complaining.

Father, son, and their dogs embark on an epic hunt. For more than two days, they track the clever bear at a relentless pace. On the night of the second day, Jody and Penny stay at the cabin of the widow Nellie Ginright, a woman Penny courted before he met Ora. Nellie is not home that night, but returns in the morning to find her visitors. Since Old Slewfoot has taken her livestock as well, she offers to let Penny and Jody use her old dugout canoe to cross the river and pick up the bear's trail.

At high noon on Christmas Eve day, Penny and Jody come upon the dogs keeping Slewfoot at bay. Penny shoots him and suddenly it's all over, Old Slewfoot is dead. Both Jody and Penny are amazed since they have hunted the bear time and again and he has given them the slip. The problem now is how to get Slewfoot's meat back to the Baxters'—the bear is huge and heavy. Eventually, Penny decides the best thing to do is to go to nearby Fort Gates for help.

As they walk along the road, the Forresters happen by, and every one of them is drunk. Penny offers them half the meat if they help him get Slewfoot home, and the Forresters agree. Buck decides that not only will they help Penny, they will also take him and Jody to Volusia. There, the Baxters can meet up with Ma—who already went ahead in the wagon as per Penny's instructions—for the church celebration. The

Forresters will join in as well. Penny worries that they will cause trouble but reluctantly accepts their help.

More Trouble in Volusia

Unfortunately, Penny's fears about how the Forresters will behave are soon realized. For starters, when they reach Volusia and join the celebration, a drunken Buck covers himself with Old Slewfoot's hide and goes into the church, frightening the entire congregation. However, this is a harmless prank, and soon everyone is enjoying the celebration. Penny and Jody both entertain questions about their great hunt. Although all are in high spirits, Jody finds himself feeling jealous when he sees Eulalie Boyles talking with another boy.

Then trouble brews in Volusia again as the Forresters learn that Oliver Hutto and his new wife, Twink, have just arrived by boat, and the bunch of them sneak off. Penny realizes they are gone and suspects they will harm Oliver, so he, Jody, Grandma, and Ma head in the Baxter wagon to Grandma's house. As they near their destination, Penny smells a fire and realizes that Grandma Hutto's house is burning.

Luckily, no one is hurt, but now Jody understands what his mother meant about the Forresters being mean and nasty. He takes the wagon to find—and warn—Oliver. Once he tracks him down, Jody tells Oliver the Forresters set fire to Grandma's house, and they all hurry back to the scene of the crime. However, when they arrive, Grandma denies the Forresters' involvement. She is a wise woman and does not want Oliver to take on the Forresters and either be killed or go to jail for killing them. Penny backs up her story and secretly tells her he wishes he had her good sense.

Although Oliver assures her he will build her a new house, Grandma refuses. She says she wants to move immediately to Boston with him (in part, to put distance between Oliver and the Forresters). On Christmas morning, the

Baxters and the Huttos say a tearful goodbye as Grandma, Oliver, and Twink set sail for Boston.

The Mischievous Flag

In February, Penny is laid up in bed with his rheumatism, and Jody notices his fawn is no longer a fawn. Flag has grown into a yearling and is still very playful. He continues to do things—accidentally—that diminish the Baxter food supply. One day he knocks over some peas that are drying and is barred from the house because he's too big and too playful. Flag also tramples Penny's prized tobacco plants. Penny says he will not tell Ma—since it was accidental—if Jody will fix up the tobacco plants that remain. Jody agrees and begins to try to think up ways to keep Flag out of trouble, but the yearling is so smart—slipping its halter and opening the pen door—he wonders if it is possible.

By March, Penny is feeling well and he and Jody begin sowing the fields. For days they work hard planting corn and other crops. One day when they are planting cow peas, Penny tries to remove a stump and injures himself. He cannot straighten up and is laid up in bed again. To make matters worse, shortly thereafter, Flag eats all the corn plants they planted. Jody tells his father and begs him not to tell Ma, but Penny says he must. After conferring with Ma, Penny tells Jody he will be allowed to keep Flag if he replants the corn and builds a six-foot fence around the field, a fence the yearling cannot jump.

Jody works diligently, replants the corn, and begins to work on the fence. As he builds the fence up to five feet at one end of the field, even Ma is impressed by how hard he works. She offers to help him build the fence a foot higher, and soon it is six feet tall. Just as he and Ma finish the fence at one end, Jody realizes the corn is breaking ground again. He tries to tie up Flag, but the clever yearling slips his halter. Jody works furiously to finish the fence before the corn comes through and tempts the yearling.

However, when the fence is nearly finished, Jody and Ma realize that six feet is not enough. Flag can still jump over the fence easily, and they cannot build a fence high enough to keep out the yearling. Thus, Flag will surely eat their food, and as a result the family may starve. According to Penny, there is only one solution: Flag must be killed to insure that the Baxters will not go hungry. He tells Jody to shoot the young deer.

The Death of the Yearling

Jody is being asked to make the ultimate sacrifice. He must give up something he loves, something that gives him comfort, for the sake of the family. Unable to face his responsibility, Jody decides he will not shoot Flag and tries everything he can think of to save him. He takes Flag to the Forresters' hoping they will keep the yearling, but the Forresters refuse. Jody then decides to take Flag to Jacksonville, but Flag is too unruly and will not follow him. Finally, Jody is forced to give up and return home at dark. He sneaks into the smokehouse with Flag and hides out for the night, but in the morning when he wakes Flag is gone.

Now there is very little hope left for the yearling. Jody hears his mother yelling. She has discovered Flag, who spent the early morning hours eating the crops for the second time. Ma sends Jody in to see his father, who sends Jody to his room. Jody hears a shot and runs out to find that Ma shot Flag, but her aim is poor and Flag is suffering badly. Flag hobbles away and Penny tells his son he must end the suffering—Penny cannot do it because he cannot walk. Jody yells that Penny has betrayed him. He tells Penny he hates him and hopes he dies. Jody takes his gun, finds Flag by the sinkhole—a special place where the two of them frequently went together—and shoots him.

Then, Jody runs away. He resolves to find Oliver in Boston and decides the best way to get there is by boat. He makes plans to paddle Nellie Ginright's small canoe down the creek until he can catch a passing steamer to Boston. For days Jody goes hungry, desperately paddling toward the St. Johns River. In the

At first, Jody cannot bring himself to shoot Flag, but he does so after a poor shot by Ma wounds the fawn.

process, he learns what starvation is, what his parents meant when they said the family would starve if Flag ate the crops. After days of very little food, Jody passes out from hunger and awakes to find himself lying in a bunk on a mail boat with two men trying to help him. The men give him soup and biscuits to strengthen him. Exhaustion, however, takes over and Jody falls asleep, waking when the boat docks at Volusia. Jody goes up onto the deck feeling better, and the captain asks where he is headed. "Boston," he replies. The captain realizes that Jody is running away and instead leaves him in Volusia.

Growing Up

There is no place left for Jody to go but home. He realizes how selfish he has been, thinking of his own needs before those of his family. He hopes his parents will take him back. Along the way he stops at the stream to build a flutter mill as he had on an April day a year ago. This time, however, the flutter mill "had lost its comfort" and seems childish to Jody. He is no longer a child.

Jody thinks of Penny and is homesick immediately. He runs home hoping Penny will take him back. Penny cries when he sees Jody. He is happy to have his beloved son back, and Jody realizes he is still wanted. He tells Penny he did not mean it when he said he hated him and assures his father he will be accepting more responsibility. Penny talks to him man to man. His speech summarizes everything that Jody learned in the past year:

> You've seed how things goes in the world o' men. You've knowed men to be low-down and mean. You've seed ol' Death at his tricks. You've messed around with ol' Starvation. Ever' man wants life to be a fine thing, and a easy. 'Tis fine boy, powerful fine, but 'tain't easy. Life knocks a man down and he gits up and it knocks him down agin.[60]

Jody knows his father is right. He saw the Forresters be low-down and mean. He saw Fodder-wing and Flag die. He knows what starvation feels like after running away to the river. He is no longer a carefree child. That night, Jody drifts off to sleep dreaming of both Flag and himself frolicking in a field. He realizes that neither the yearling nor the child exists anymore. Jody has grown up.

CHAPTER FOUR

The Characters

The plot of *The Yearling* centers around three principal families: the Baxters, the Forresters, and the Huttos. It is through the interactions of individual members of each of these clans that Jody learns the lessons necessary for him to achieve adulthood.

The Baxters

A small family of three, the Baxters live on a hundred-acre farm in the Florida scrub. They purchased the land from their closest neighbors, the Forresters, who live four miles away. Their property—called Baxter's Island—is described as "high good land in the center of a pine island."[61] However, the word *island* does not mean that the Baxters' land is surrounded by water; rather, it is a mass of long-leaf pine trees surrounded by scrub land.

On this land they eke out a subsistence living. Penny hunts for game, raises livestock, and plants crops of corn and sweet potatoes. He and Jody haul water to the house from a nearby sinkhole that lies on the edge of the property. Essentially, the Baxters are hardworking, good-living frontier people making do the best they can in the sparsely populated scrub.

Ezra Ezekial "Penny" Baxter

Although Ezra Ezekial Baxter is a man in his fifties, he is no bigger than a boy. It was Lem Forrester who nicknamed him "Penny" because of his size—no bigger than a penny-piece—and the name stuck. Penny grew up on a small farm near Volusia, Florida, and has done backbreaking work from the time he was a boy. His father was a stern preacher and taught him the Scriptures as well as how to read and write. In his thirties he married Ora Alvers and moved them to high land surrounded by scrub, which he named Baxter's Island.

Rawlings never explains precisely what happened to Penny that hurt him so badly that he wished to leave civilization. The reader knows only that Penny was somehow hurt by living amid people, that he craves solitude and does not like any intrusion on his individual spirit. Rawlings alludes to the fact that Penny has been severely injured by life, saying that "he had perhaps been bruised too often. The peace of the vast aloof scrub had drawn him with the beneficence of its silence. . . . The forays of bear and wolf and wild-cat and panther on stock were understandable, which was more than he could say of human cruelties."[62]

Still, Penny dealt with more sadness once he moved to the scrub. He hoped for a big family, but all but one of his children died soon after birth. At least five Baxter children died before Jody survived. When Jody was two, Penny enlisted in the Confederate army, took his wife and child to live with Grandma Hutto, and went off to fight the Civil War. He returned four years later to the isolation of the scrub for peace and solitude. The death of his children and his stint in the war contributed to the heavy burden that Penny carries with him.

Penny has been called Rawlings's "spokesman" by many critics who believe it is his ideology she was trying to convey. Penny knows about the habits of animals and is renowned for his hunting skill, but he hates to kill. He lives by a strict moral code and is the epitome of a good, noble man.

Penny adores his son Jody and is determined to teach him the ways of men: how to hunt, trade, and support a family. Penny sees himself in his son and wants to allow Jody to have the childhood he never had. Since Flag is an important part of this childhood, Penny protects the fawn from Ma Baxter. He insists that she not complain about the food used to feed the newest Baxter and even covers up some of Flag's accidents. But as Jody passes from boyhood to manhood, Penny passes from good health to decay. As a result, he is forced to give up some of the adult responsibilities around the Baxter home and can no longer protect Jody from having his "guts tore out" by the realities of the world. Eventually, when Flag's accidents threaten the family's well-being, Penny's adult responsibility to provide for his family takes precedence over his desire to protect Jody's boyhood. Penny must order Jody to shoot the fawn he loves so that the Baxters will not go hungry.

Jody Baxter

Jody Baxter is the protagonist of *The Yearling*, and the story details his growth from childhood to young adulthood. He is small like his father, has blue eyes, a pale, freckled face, and straw-colored, shaggy hair with drakes tails in the back. Jody calls himself ugly and wishes he were handsome like his hero and best friend Oliver Hutto, who assures him he will be.

Jody can barely read or write, but this is due to a lack of schooling, not a lack of intelligence. It is difficult to get a formal education in the sparsely populated scrub, and most of what Jody knows he learned either from a teacher the Forresters and Baxters boarded one winter or from his father. However, Jody's inherent intelligence can be seen in his sensitive understanding of the animals and vegetation of the scrub.

Jody learned about nature, hunting, and fishing from Penny and has a very special relationship with his father. He idolizes Penny and dreams of being noble and good like him in his adult years. Penny is the nurturing and protective force in

Jody idolizes his father, who is the nurturing force in the boy's life.

Jody's life. However, while Penny works to protect Jody's childhood innocence, Ma Baxter wants to end it prematurely. As a result, Jody's relationship with her is strained. Ma Baxter is not a warm and nurturing mother, but a distant and cold one. She constantly nags him to grow up and belittles him for not accepting enough adult responsibility.

Although he may not meet his mother's standards for responsibility, for the most part Jody is a well-mannered boy, and he listens to his parents. However, there are a few exceptions, the most notable being his potato assault on Eulalie Boyles. Throughout the novel Jody is confused about his feelings for Eulalie. In their meeting at Boyles's store, he translates his confusion into anger and throws a potato at her. Later, a more mature Jody realizes he is jealous when he sees Eulalie with another boy.

Throughout the novel Jody longs for a pet of his own, something that will love him and depend on him. Finally, he is able to have one, a fawn named Flag that becomes his constant companion. Penny quickly realizes how important Flag is to Jody and protects the fawn from Ma Baxter's ire. However, when Flag's antics threaten the Baxters' food supply, Penny must order Jody to shoot the deer to ensure the family's survival.

Jody does not understand why Flag must be killed and runs away after shooting the yearling. On his journey, he realizes the ways in which Flag's behavior threatened his family and concludes that he was selfishly putting his needs before his family's survival. However, Jody also recognizes that he will never feel the carefree safety of childhood again now that he comprehends the cruelty of survival. Essentially, the incident forces Jody to accept the responsibilities of young adulthood. At the end of the book, he is no longer the child he was at the beginning.

Ora Alvers "Ma" Baxter

"Ma" Baxter is a pioneer woman through and through. A big, broad woman, she is twice Penny's size. She lives with very few conveniences—not even a well by the house to make the laundry easier. She is a good cook of the little food the family has, and keeps the Baxter home clean and neat.

Ma has very little compassion or sympathy for anyone and is quick to think the worst of them. She looks down on anyone who does not live up to her standards and dislikes almost everyone with whom she has contact. She despises the Forresters, who she believes are wicked and "black-hearted," and condemns Grandma Hutto for living a life with too many frills.

As far as her own family goes, she seems to love both Penny and Jody in her own way. However, Penny is too compassionate for her liking and in her opinion he allows Jody to get away with too much. Ma nags Jody and has a sharp tongue that frequently lashes out at either him or his father. However, despite her complaining about others, Ma never makes a fuss about things she does not have, and is overjoyed when Penny buys her fabric and buttons for a new Christmas dress.

The source of Ma's disagreeable disposition is the great deal of sadness she has had in her life. She lost many children and, in a reflective moment, tells Penny this is what makes her so unsympathetic to her fellow human beings. Rawlings implies that this is also the reason why she has such a poor relationship with her son. Early on in the novel, the reader is told that Ma accepts "her youngest with something of a detachment, as though she had given all she had of love and care and interest"[63] to the children who came before him and died.

Flag

When Penny nearly dies of a snakebite, he kills a doe and uses her organs to save himself. Although Penny survives, the doe's fawn is left without a mother, and Penny allows Jody to keep the young deer as a pet. Since a "fawn's tail's a leetle merry white flag,"[64] Jody's friend Fodder-wing names him Flag. Because the Baxters live a rather isolated life out in the scrub, Flag becomes Jody's constant companion. Jody loves him, tells him secrets, sleeps with him, dotes on him, and cares for him.

However, as Flag grows from a fawn into a yearling, he begins to cause trouble on the Baxter farm. In his playfulness he accidentally does things that threaten the Baxters' food supply. When he is a big strong yearling, there is clearly no longer any way to contain him since he can open doors, slip ties, and get into anything. One day when the Baxters' corn plants break ground, he eats them all, and the situation becomes dire. If the corn cannot grow, the Baxters will go hungry in the winter.

The solution is to protect the corn plants from Flag, and therefore Jody tries to build a fence around the cornfield. However, the Baxters soon realize that Flag will easily jump over any fence they can build. Since there is no longer any other way to keep him from eating the corn, Penny orders Jody to shoot Flag. When Flag dies, Jody feels betrayed by his father, who had previously protected the animal from Ma's wrath by keeping some "accidents" a secret but then insisted the yearling be shot.

Jody runs away, but eventually returns to the scrub when he realizes that Penny made the right—although difficult—choice. Jody recognizes that Flag's death was a sacrifice he had to make for the greater good of the family. He is now ready to accept a more adult role in the family. Thus, it is Flag's death that forces Jody to mature to young adulthood.

The Forresters

The Forresters live four miles away and are the Baxters' closest neighbors. It is suggested that the family moved to the scrub because they are a "family of great burly quarrelsome males" that "needed all the room in the county."[65] They live in a cabin that is always alive with the sounds of booming voices and activity. Ma and Pa Forrester are a "wizened" old pair who raised seven sons: Fodder-wing, Lem, Buck, Mill-Wheel, Gabby, Pack, and Arch. They all live rough and easy, not worrying about hygiene and making money any way they can.

Critic Samuel I. Bellman suggests there is a mirror image between the Baxters and the Forresters. He writes, "Fodderwing, a saintly child who loved all the animals of the scrub, was the seventh Forrester son and the only one too frail to survive. Jody Baxter, the last of the seven or so Baxter offspring, was the only one hardy enough to survive."[66] This connection is alluded to by Ma Forrester after Fodder-wing's death when she remarks to Jody, "I been standin' here thinkin' about your Ma. She's burrit as many as I got."[67]

Buck Forrester

Even Ma Baxter, who vehemently dislikes the Forresters, has to admit that Buck is a good man. Penny agrees, telling Jody at one point in the novel that "Buck's the only one o' the litter [of Forresters] was wuth raisin'. Him and pore Fodderwing."[68] Compared with his reckless, rough, and unruly brothers (except for Fodder-wing), Buck is a gentle, reasonable, and responsible man. However, he is also very much part of the Forrester family. He is big, bearded, and hairy like all the Forrester brothers. He drinks—and perhaps assists in making—moonshine, and he makes his living "rough and easy."

Buck is the most good-natured and boisterous of the Forrester brothers. He likes to keep on the move, coming and going as he pleases. He is loyal to his brothers and fights for them, as he does with Lem against Oliver Hutto. Buck is also a bit mischievous. It is a drunken Buck who wears Old Slewfoot's hide into the Christmas festivities and frightens the crowd. In fact, when he's drunk, he can be a bit ornery and lose some of his good sense. This is certainly the case when the Forrester brothers burn down Grandma Hutto's house.

However, Buck is also trustworthy and level-headed. He sees Lem's faults—his meanness and the way he picks fights and holds a grudge—and does not get caught up in hating the Baxters or doing them harm. There is a gentle, caring side to Buck, as evinced when a rattlesnake bites Penny and Buck puts personal differences aside to assist the Baxters. Also, when Jody is frightened, Buck reassures him that they will do what they can to save his ailing father. While Penny is laid up ill from the snakebite, it is Buck who stays and works the Baxter farm. But Buck's tenderness is best displayed during the time of Fodder-wing's death. It is then that he comforts and holds Jody and volunteers to carry Fodder-wing's coffin alone.

Perhaps because of all Buck's good qualities, Buck is the only Forrester that Penny trusts. Of all the Forresters, Buck is the closest to believing Penny's ethics of hunting. At one point, Penny tells Jody that he should kill only the animals he needs to survive and that killing just to kill is evil. When Penny goes hunting with the Forresters, they all kill wantonly, especially Lem. Buck, noting Penny's displeasure at Lem's destructive attitudes, tries to keep his brother in check.

Fodder-wing Forrester

Fodder-wing is the youngest son of the Forrester family. Unlike his burly, healthy brothers, he is crippled and frail. Fodder-wing is considered "witless" by adults. He got his name because he believed that if he attached something light and airy to his body, he could jump off the roof and float gently to the ground. He tied a great deal of fodder to himself and leapt only to crash to the ground.

The entire Forrester family adores Fodder-wing, as does Jody, who considers him to be his second best friend next to Oliver Hutto. Fodder-wing is kind and gentle. He keeps a variety of animals as pets (he has a way with animals) and also tells tall tales.

In the year the book covers, Fodder-wing dies and it is his passing that gives Jody insight into the nature of death. Fodder-wing's death hits the Forresters very hard since he holds a special place in their hearts. Pa Forrester remarks that it would have been easier to have lost any one of the physically strong, healthy

The death of Fodder-wing (right) affects Jody (left) deeply.

Forrester children. Thus, through Fodder-wing's death, the reader sees a kinder, gentler side to the Forrester family, and understands that the measure of a person is not merely their physical appearance or prowess. This frail boy brought his family members more kindness and joy than any of his brothers.

Lem Forrester

Lem is a tall, lean mountain man. He resembles his brothers but is thinner than the rest and the only one without a beard. His personality also differs. He is described as a bit of a loner, brooding and sulky. Over the course of the novel, he is revealed to be the meanest and most quarrelsome Forrester and is the source of many problems and conflicts. Buck suggests various reasons for his brother's foul disposition, telling Penny early on that "Lem's different. He takes things personal."[69] Later in the story, Buck implies that Lem has become even more combative since he lost Twink to Oliver.

Whatever the reason, Lem is the most rotten apple in the Forrester bunch. It is Lem who coaxes his brothers into ganging up on Oliver Hutto and holds a grudge toward Penny and Jody after they come to Oliver's rescue. When relations between the Forresters and the Baxters improve again, Lem gets bent out of shape about a buck that Penny shoots and threatens to fight him. Finally, when Oliver and Twink marry and return to Volusia, a drunken group of Forresters—the reader assumes they are led by Lem—burns down Grandma Hutto's house on Christmas Eve.

While all of these actions seem to prove what Ma, Penny, and even Lem's brothers have said all along—Lem is just plain ornery and unkind—it is a hunting incident that best illustrates Lem's pure meanness. When the Forrester brothers, Penny, and Jody capture the bear cubs on their hunt, Rawlings describes Lem's interaction with a cub: "Lem picked up a stick and began to tease one of the cubs. He poked it in the ribs to make it bite the stick. He knocked it over and it squealed in pain."[70] Eventually, Lem "torments" the bear cub to such a degree that Penny and Buck are forced to intervene and suggest that he either kill it or leave it be.

Mill-Wheel Forrester

Mill-Wheel lies somewhere in between Lem and Buck in terms of personality and character. He is as bearded and big as the other Forrester brothers. He is described as boisterous and enjoys carousing, dancing, playing music, moonshining, and rough and easy living. However, Mill-Wheel is neither as mean as Lem nor as good as Buck.

Ma Forrester

Ma Forrester is the matriarch of the Forrester clan and has her boys doing whatever she wants—even washing dishes, something considered "women's work" in Jody's home. She is a vivacious, loud, and boisterous woman who smells of snuff and wood smoke. It is Ma who remembers that Fodder-wing named the fawn Flag before he died, and thereby gives Jody a sense of closure about his friend's death.

Pa Forrester

Quieter and more reserved than his wife, Pa Forrester is a wise man who occasionally says insightful things to Jody. It is Pa who notices the irony of the family's grief in losing Fodder-wing—namely, that while Fodder-wing was physically not as useful as his brothers, he meant more to everyone than his brothers did. However, most of the time, the wise and soft-spoken old man is ignored in the Forrester home, overpowered by his loud and vivacious wife and sons.

Grandma Hutto

Grandma Hutto is a small, plump, vivacious woman with a mind of her own. Grandma smells of lavender and flowers and has locks of silver curls falling about a shining pink face and black eyes. She lives in a small white cottage with a white picket fence and a beautiful flower garden that lies on the bank of the St. Johns River in Volusia.

Grandma is a longtime friend of Penny Baxter, and Ma Baxter and two-year-old Jody lived with her while Penny went off to fight in the Civil War. While Jody grew to love Grandma in the four years Penny was away, Ora Baxter grew to dislike her because of her "frilliness."

However, there is another possible reason for Ma's antagonism toward Grandma. Although she is a widow, Grandma has a way with men that makes them adore her—young and old alike. Rawlings writes, "Something about her was forever female and made all men virile."[71] The reader learns that this quality also makes some women dislike her, and it appears that Ma Baxter is one such woman.

Her handyman, Easy Ozell, courts Grandma throughout the novel, but she will have nothing to do with a Yankee. Instead, she focuses her attention on her son, Oliver, whom she fusses over when he returns home from the sea. When the feud between Oliver and Lem escalates and her house is burnt to the ground, Grandma's good sense prevails. She lies to Oliver, telling him that the Forresters were not at fault, and then insists that she move to Boston immediately. This way, Oliver will not be in danger of a violent confrontation with the Forresters.

Oliver Hutto

Oliver is Grandma Hutto's son. He has gray-blue eyes, a great smile, and a lean body. Jody idolizes Oliver and considers him his best friend. Since he is a sailor, Oliver often regales friends and family with exciting tales of exotic places. When he comes home to see his mother, Oliver wears hoop earrings and his hair is bleached and his skin bronzed from all the time he has spent in the sun. This only enhances his good looks.

Oliver's girlfriend is Twink Weatherby. However, when he goes off to sea, Lem Forrester begins to covet Twink's attention.

This ignites a feud between Oliver and the Forrester brothers that forces young Jody to choose sides and, eventually, see the unkindness of people. He recognizes this unkindness when the Forresters set fire to Grandma Hutto's home and Jody is forced to concede that Ma Baxter was right all along—the Forresters are simply mean spirited.

Minor Characters

There are quite a few residents of the town of Volusia with whom Jody comes into contact once or twice in *The Yearling*. Though they may not play large roles in the novel, it is never-theless important to understand these characters. Specifically, it is worthwhile to realize what they contribute to the events of the book and to explain their relationships with Jody and each other.

Eulalie Boyles

Eulalie is Mr. Boyles's niece, and the girl whom Jody has a crush on, though he pretends to hate her. She has a lean, lank body, a freckled face, squirrel teeth (according to Jody), and wears her hair in pigtails. Jody sees her twice in the novel, and his reactions to her illustrate his growing maturity in dealing with his feelings toward the opposite sex. The first time Jody and Eulalie interact, he acts very childishly, throwing a potato at her out of anger and confusion. However, when he sees her much later in the novel, she is with another boy, and Jody quickly realizes that he is jeal-ous of the boy who gets to spend time with Eulalie.

Mr. Boyles

Mr. Boyles is the proprietor of the store in Volusia where Penny does his trading. He is described as being as honest as Penny himself. Boyles is considered "judge and arbiter and encyclope-dia"[72] for the small town of Volusia. He is kind enough to offer to give Jody a harmonica, but Jody has to give it back after he throws a potato at Eulalie Boyles, Mr. Boyles's niece.

Nellie Ginright

Before Penny married Jody's mother, Ora Alvers, he courted Nellie Ginright, who broke off their courtship to date another man. Now Nellie is a middle-aged widow and wonders if she made a mistake not encouraging Penny to marry her, but that's in the past. When Penny and Jody track Old Slewfoot for three days, they spend one night at Nellie's home. She is away for the night but returns in the morning, and she and Penny sit laughing and talking over breakfast.

Nellie is pretty, jovial, plump, and rosy. Jody believes she is of Grandma Hutto's "breed" of women, the kind that makes men feel at ease. In the end, it turns out that Old Slewfoot has been bothering her as well, and she gives Penny and Jody her old, leaky canoe to pursue the bear. It is this same canoe that Jody patches to use when he tries to run away to Boston.

Old Slewfoot

Old Slewfoot is the nickname of a giant bear who has been troubling both the Baxters and the Forresters—and numerous others—for years. He got his name because of his irregular right foot that is missing one toe. The giant bear preys on farmers' livestock, killing the Baxters' sow early in the novel and returning toward the end to claim a calf. The bear proves a worthy opponent for Penny, who is known as the best hunter in the scrub. The clever animal continually eludes both traps and the great hunter throughout most of the novel. However, when Old Slewfoot kills the Baxters' calf, Penny and Jody set out on an epic hunt to kill the bear. It takes them nearly three days to track him, but the actual kill is surprisingly easy.

Easy Ozell

Easy is an admirer of Grandma Hutto who fought for the Union in the Civil War. He has long, gray hair that droops on his neck and a droopy mustache to match. His arms hang limp at his sides, his feet drag, and he's bow-legged. He works for Grandma

Hutto—chopping wood and taking care of things around her house. He would like to date her, but she only pities him and does not want to be his girl—especially because she still holds a grudge against Yankees. Easy is humble and shy, and he gets very nervous when he tries to talk to Grandma Hutto.

Twink Weatherby

Twink is beautiful, with soft yellow curls that fall around a small, pointed white face with wide blue eyes. She is an orphan who has never had a lot in life. Twink is Oliver Hutto's girl-friend, but when he goes away to sea, Lem Forrester begins to believe that she is his. Throughout the novel Oliver and Lem fight over her, and the feuding men cause a great deal of trouble for the Baxters, since they are forced to choose sides. When Penny and Jody side with Oliver in the fight, the Forresters become so angry that they eventually try to steal the Baxter hogs to get revenge. Then, when Twink marries Oliver toward the end of the book, the Forresters burn down Grandma Hutto's home in retaliation.

Jody has never understood what Oliver sees in Twink, and he blames her for the trouble between the Forresters and the Baxters. However, when Oliver, Grandma, and Twink leave for Boston, Twink gives Jody a kiss and he finds it strangely agreeable. In his newfound maturity, he begins to comprehend the allure of women.

Doc Wilson

The doctor who lives closest to the Baxters, Doc Wilson, cares for Penny when he is bitten by a rattlesnake. Doc drinks heavily, and everyone, including Doc, jokes about it. But when he is at the Baxters' home caring for Penny, it is the soberest that Jody has ever seen him. He stays the night, nursing Penny and trying to save him. In the morning, he asks for no payment, but Jody gives him a cherished knapsack to thank him anyway.

CHAPTER FIVE

Literary Criticism

T*he Yearling* has received surprisingly little critical attention over the years, especially considering its popularity.
Two books make up the majority of criticism written
about the classic. The first of these is *Marjorie Kinnan
Rawlings* by Samuel I. Bellman. Published in 1974, the author
relates the characters and ideology in *The Yearling* to Marjorie
Kinnan Rawlings's personal life. The second book is Gordon E.
Bigelow's *Frontier Eden,* which examines Rawlings's literary
career. Bigelow focuses on very different topics than Bellman
does, including style, structure, and the genres of literature with
which *The Yearling* is associated. These two works, and addi-
tional articles, make up the body of criticism surrounding *The
Yearling.* Most importantly, they provide valuable insight into
the meaning of the work.

Realism

Critics place *The Yearling* in a variety of categories, or genres,
of fiction. One such category is realism. The term *realism*
refers to a style of fiction that presents a fictional world that
seems as though it is the one in which the reader lives. Human
characters in a novel of this type resemble people readers meet

in daily life. They are not superhuman or less than human; these characters possess good points as well as faults. Some behave nobly and others reprehensibly.

In the case of animal characters, Lucille W. Van Vliet's discussion of the way in which animals are portrayed in realistic fiction is helpful. She states that, in this category of fiction, "animals behave like animals. . . . They are not given the power of speech or humanized. Characteristics and behavior of animals are realistically described."[73] Certainly this is true for Flag as well as the other animals in *The Yearling*.

Although the events of the novel are realistic—the Baxters' adventures and trials seem as though they really could occur in the 1870s Florida scrub—a realistic plot is not required for a novel to be considered realistic fiction. What is important is the way in which the story is told, the author's writing style. In a realistic novel, the author reports events matter-of-factly and therefore the events of the novel seem, in M. H. Abrams's words, "the very stuff of ordinary experience."[74] Early critics alluded to Rawlings's realistic writing style, referring to the book as a "beautifully composed record of a year's living"[75] or a "simple chronicle."[76]

Thus, *The Yearling* is definitely an example of realistic fiction. However, Gordon E. Bigelow is even more specific. He argues that it represents a certain type of realism, one that Rawlings used in many of her works, not only those written for younger readers. He considers it a "brightly lighted," "cleaned-up realism which [leaves out] the sordid and most forms of the ugly." According to Bigelow, that which Rawlings presents, she presents realistically; however, she leaves out many things that are part of everyday life for most people: sexual experience, social intercourse, politics, education, government, and religion. Thus, hers is a restricted realism. To clarify, Bigelow writes, "[American poet] Robert Frost spoke of two kinds of realist in literature, the one who offers a good deal of dirt with his potato to show that it is a real potato, and the one who is satisfied with the potato brushed clean. Marjorie was a realist of the second kind."[77]

Regionalism

In its April 4, 1938, issue, *Time* magazine commented on Rawlings's "excellent descriptions of Florida scrub landscapes" and "skillful use of the native vernacular"[78] in *The Yearling*. Comments such as these point to a subgenre of realism of which *The Yearling* is representative: regional literature. Regional literature tries to accurately reflect the geography and environment of a particular region or locale as well as faithfully document the history, speech, dress, and general way of life of its inhabitants.

The region Rawlings depicts in *The Yearling* is a portion of northern Florida known as the scrub. She clarifies where it is located—near the St. Johns River by Volusia—and the types of vegetation and wildlife that exist in this region. Her characters speak in the dialect of the 1870s scrub, and the reader glimpses their way of life, from what they eat to the types of homes they live in. Therefore, *The Yearling* can be placed squarely in the category of regional literature.

Regional literature achieved great popularity in the late 1920s and the 1930s. Thus, at the time *The Yearling* was published, Rawlings was one of many authors writing regionalist novels. She was also one of numerous authors to win the Pulitzer Prize for a regional novel during this time. Writers such as William Faulkner, John Steinbeck, and Ellen Glasgow also received this accolade for their work in bringing a particular region of the country to life. Ironically, Rawlings disliked the term *regional literature* and argued that "the phrase 'regional literature' . . . is not only false and unsound but dangerous" because its popularity at the time led to the publication of books simply because they were regional and not because they were good literature. However, she also agreed that there was some "valid" regional literature—novels written by a "sincere creative writer who has something to say" and sets the story in a specific region. This type of good regional literature, according to Rawlings, "is only incidentally, sometimes even accidentally, regional."[79]

Whether she liked the term or not, Rawlings's most famous work, *The Yearling,* is considered one of the premier pieces of regional literature. As a result, she will most often be referred to as a regionalist. Gordon Bigelow may have said it best when he claimed that "fame has many faces, but fame for Marjorie Kinnan Rawlings wears the lean tanned features of a Florida cracker . . . and it is primarily as a regionalist that she will be remembered."[80]

Nature and Romance

One of the things that Rawlings loved best about her region of the country was the wilderness that surrounded her, especially the scrub. It is therefore not surprising that nature is such an important aspect of *The Yearling.* It is almost a character unto itself. In his critical work, Gordon Bigelow attempts to explain nature and the wilderness in the story. He contends that Rawlings strikes a balance between a romantic and realistic style in her discussion of nature. It is romantic because nature is presented as strange and unique, and the book is focused around it. Here, romance does not refer to people falling in love but, instead, to a genre of poetry and fiction. For the purposes of understanding Bigelow's comments, it is only necessary to understand that romantic literature frequently focuses on the description of a beautiful, idealized nature. *The Yearling* does have some beautiful, mystical, romantic nature scenes. One such scene occurs when Jody and Penny watch the whooping cranes dance. Rawlings wrote,

> The setting sun lay rosy on the white bodies [of the cranes]. Magic birds were dancing in a mystic marsh. The grass swayed with them, and the shallow waters, and the earth fluttered under them. The earth was dancing with the cranes, and the low sun, and the wind and sky.[81]

However, all is not always beautiful and strange in Rawlings's natural wilderness because, as Bigelow astutely points out, Rawlings is also a realist. He writes, "because she wished to tell the whole truth, the nature she depicts has not only idyllic beauty, as in the episode where Jody Baxter makes his flutter mill at Silver Glen Springs; it also has terror, as when Penny is struck by a rattlesnake, and an inscrutable cruelty, as when the great storm destroys the Baxters' crops."[82] Thus, the nature she depicts in the story—while primarily beautiful—is also dangerous and terrifying, reflecting the unpredictable and indifferent quality that is inherent to a realist presentation.

Various critics maintain that Rawlings's own belief in the importance of people finding their place in nature heavily influenced her writing. She believed that people's relationships to their surroundings were as important as their relationships to other people. In her view, there was a particular environment in which each individual would be happy—one person may be happy in the mountains, while another enjoys the sea. In order to be happy, a person must discover which environment is right for him or her. The more natural the setting of this environment, the happier he or she will be.

Critic Lamar York maintains that Rawlings uses rivers in her works to illustrate this philosophy that "a man must know or discover a relationship to a suitable physical setting." According to York, in *The Yearling*, the St. Johns River helps Jody discover the environment in which he belongs and can be happy. Throughout the book, the river symbolizes the outer edge of the scrub, which is Jody's world. It is a limit circumscribing his physical home and his mental childhood. Near the end of the story, Jody has run away and is on the river attempting to go to Boston. Thus, the river is also a gateway to other places. York contends that when Jody is alone on the river toward the end of the novel, he is in limbo between the scrub where he has lived his whole life and the greater world symbolized by Boston. Moreover, "he is at [a crossroads], between his old childlike acceptance of life as a sure thing and his coming reconciliation with his adult role in the scrub homestead." It is here on the river that he discovers the environment in which he will be happy. He comes to understand that "he will not find himself by getting away from the scrub."[83] He returns home to his proper place and tells his father he wishes to make his home in the scrub.

The Message: Sentimental or Nightmarish?

One of the few disagreements critics have about *The Yearling* regards its overall message. In an early review of *The Yearling*, Jonathan Daniels told potential readers it was a good book, but "it falters occasionally into sentimentality" and "sometimes seems artificial and shaped for [a] trivial story."[84] Nearly thirty years later in an extensive examination of Pulitzer Prize–winning novels, W. J. Stuckey found *The Yearling* "too slight and sentimental. . . ."[85]

However, other critics argue the exact opposite, maintaining that the book is "never sentimental."[86] Samuel I. Bellman even asserts that serious readers—Daniels and Stuckey considered among them—have been misled by the "surface sentimentality" of *The Yearling*. The story does not send a sappy, sentimental message but, instead, "echoes a frightened and lost child crying into the night, out of fear, disappointment, and despair."[87]

Thus, critics line up in opposite camps to debate whether the book is merely sentimental. A great deal is actually at stake. Critics such as Stuckey who conclude that the book is sappy frequently argue that it does not "merit serious attention."[88] Those in the Bellman camp, however, suggest that the book has been foolishly overlooked and ignored by critics.

Examining Jody Baxter

Readers enjoy *The Yearling* because they have an affection for Jody Baxter. They care what happens to him. When Flag dies, it is not only Jody who feels sadness. Many readers of *The Yearling* are sad with him. He is unanimously adored by critics, who put their pens to paper trying to explain exactly what it is about Jody Baxter that makes him so lovable.

William Soskin asserts that it is Jody's personality that endears him to the reader, especially his "sensitive emotional understanding" of animals, "wholesomeness" of spirit, and "bubbling humor."[89] Samuel I. Bellman contends that an examination of Rawlings's own life provides a key psychological reason for Jody's universal appeal. He argues

The wholesome, sensitive, and lovable character of Jody played a large part in making The Yearling *a classic.*

it is Rawlings's "profound sympathy" for Jody that makes him such a wonderful character. According to Bellman, this sympathy results from the fact that Jody is the "finest and most heartwarming expression of the boy she had always wanted but never had."[90] Bellman delves into her life and writings to illustrate that Rawlings's childlessness left her feeling unfulfilled, and he suggests that she was able to find fulfillment in her work by describing the nurturing of a boy, Jody Baxter. In his opinion, this character is her ultimate achievement.

Style and Structure

William Soskin writes, "It is because we have known the innermost recesses of Jody's heart and the intimacy of his dreams that the ultimate need to kill the fawn becomes a drama of overpowering proportions."[91] In other words, it is the reader's understanding of Jody's mind and heart that makes the book work.

In *Frontier Eden,* Bigelow explores the style and structure that Rawlings uses to create Jody's consciousness. Bigelow claims the story is written "chiefly as a sequence of revelations to the alert, yet open and wondering mind of twelve-year-old Jody Baxter." This is not accomplished through the first person—the reader is not hearing Jody's thoughts directly. Instead, *The Yearling* is written in a modified third person. According to Bigelow, this allows Rawlings to be highly selective. At any moment she could choose between showing exactly what Jody was thinking, presenting an edited version of his thoughts as well as a reaction to some impression, or leaving Jody's mind altogether and commenting on the situation. Bigelow concludes that "her use of point of view accords perfectly with the tone she meant to strike between realistic presentation of an actual world with its sights sounds and smells, and an idyllic sense of wonder with which a twelve-year-old boy looked out upon the world."[92]

Penny Baxter's Philosophy

In her book *Marjorie Kinnan Rawlings: Sojourner at Cross Creek,* Elizabeth Silverthorne writes that the character of Penny Baxter was based on "the father of her friend Cal Long," though he also "had many of the qualities of Rawlings's own father."[93] Rawlings frequently called Penny Baxter her "spokesman" in *The Yearling,* and through him she was able to express her philosophy. According to critics, the philosophy he reveals has primarily two aspects, the first of which is his relationship with his son. Bellman returns to his analysis of Rawlings's own life to describe her characters. He comments that Penny's "profound attachment to his only son Jody . . . linked him with Mrs. Rawlings,"[94] who had always wanted a child. Christine McDonnell adds that Penny's "fathering of Jody is rich and reliable"[95] and one of the reasons that the reader enjoys the character of Penny.

Bellman and McDonnell contend that the second aspect of Penny's—and Rawlings's—philosophy is a stoic acceptance of life's hardships. These critics both quote a passage toward the end of the novel in which they believe Penny reveals this doctrine. When Jody returns home after he has run away, Penny tells his son that "life knocks a man down and he gits up and it knocks him down agin. . . . What's he to do when he gits knocked down? Why, take it for his share and go on."[96] Bellman calls this Rawlings's "tragic-stoic" view, and McDonnell submits that this attitude is "powerful in its compassion and in its determination to survive"[97] and makes the book intriguing and beautiful for adult readers.

The Symbolism of the Fawn

Various critics have noted the symbolism of the relationship between Jody and Flag. In her review of the book, Edith H. Walton details parts of their interconnectedness. She points out that, as the seasons go by and the year progresses, suddenly "the fawn is a yearling . . . almost fully grown, just as Jody himself is no longer really a child." She adds that, in the end, "the heedless boy Jody, has died with Flag, the fawn."[98]

William Soskin also noted the relationship between the end of Jody's childhood and the end of Flag's life. He wrote, "As a result of the death of the fawn young Jody comes eventually to know that his yearling days are over, as are his pet's."[99] Indeed, this seems to be the message in the final passage of the book where Rawlings writes, "Somewhere beyond the sink-hole, past the magnolia, under the live oaks, a boy and a yearling ran side by side, and were forever gone."[100] However, while most critics agree that Flag is a symbol of Jody's childhood, not all of them believe that Rawlings successfully deals with this symbolism in the novel. Stuckey maintains that it is "a rather amateurish attempt to give the story implications larger than it can bear."[101]

Notes

Introduction: *The Yearling* Experience

1. W. J. Stuckey, *The Pulitzer Prize Novels: A Critical Backward Look*. Norman: University of Oklahoma Press, 1966, p. 117.

2. Gordon E. Bigelow, *Frontier Eden: The Literary Career of Marjorie Kinnan Rawlings*. Gainesville: University of Florida Press, 1966, p. 154.

3. Jonathan Daniels, "Boy in the Backwoods," *Saturday Review of Literature*, April 2, 1938, p. 5.

4. Edith H. Walton, "A Novel of Backwoods Living," *New York Times Book Review*, April 3, 1938, p. 2.

5. William Soskin, "A Tom Sawyer of the Florida Scrub Lands," *New York Herald Tribune Books*, April 3, 1938, p. 1.

6. Bigelow, *Frontier Eden*, p. 137.

7. Samuel I. Bellman, *Marjorie Kinnan Rawlings*. New York: Twayne, 1974, p. 54.

8. Rodger L. Tarr, ed., *Max and Marjorie: The Correspondence Between Maxwell E. Perkins and Marjorie Kinnan Rawlings*. Gainesville: University Press of Florida, 1999, pp. 22–23.

9. Christine McDonnell, "A Second Look: *The Yearling*," *Horn Book Magazine*, June 1977, pp. 344–45.

10. Bigelow, *Frontier Eden*, p. 158.

Chapter 1: The Life of Marjorie Kinnan Rawlings

11. Quoted in Tarr, *Max and Marjorie*, p. 117.

12. Quoted in Gordon E. Bigelow and Laura V. Monti, eds., *Selected Letters of Marjorie Kinnan Rawlings*. Gainesville: University Presses of Florida, 1983, p. 92.

13. Bigelow, *Frontier Eden*, p. 157.

14. Quoted in Tarr, *Max and Marjorie*, p. 36.

15. Percy Hutchison, "Backwater Life in Florida's 'Scrub,'" *New York Times Book Review*, March 5, 1933, p. 7.

16. Herschel Brickell, "Florida Crackers in the Sandy Florida Scrub," *New York Herald Tribune Books*, March 5, 1933, p. 5.

17. Quoted in Bigelow and Monti, *Selected Letters of Marjorie Kinnan Rawlings,* p. 90.

18. Quoted in Bigelow and Monti, *Selected Letters of Marjorie Kinnan Rawlings,* p. 80.

19. Percy Hutchison, "A Novel of the People in Florida's Swamps," *New York Times Book Review,* October 6, 1935, p. 3.

20. Idella Parker, with Mary Keating, *Idella: Marjorie Kinnan Rawlings' "Perfect Maid."* Gainesville: University Press of Florida, 1992, pp. 74–75.

21. Quoted in Bigelow and Monti, *Selected Letters of Marjorie Kinnan Rawlings,* p. 214.

22. Parker, *Idella,* p. 95.

23. Rose Feld, "Marjorie Rawlings and Her Neighbors," *New York Herald Tribune Books,* March 15, 1942, p. 1.

24. Quoted in Elizabeth Silverthorne, *Marjorie Kinnan Rawlings: Sojourner at Cross Creek.* Woodstock, NY: Overlook Press, 1988, p. 220.

25. Quoted in Silverthorne, *Marjorie Kinnan Rawlings,* p. 250.

26. Parker, *Idella,* pp. 104–105.

27. Louis Bromfield, "Case of Wandering the Wits," *Saturday Review,* January 4, 1953, p. 10.

Chapter 2: The History of *The Yearling*

28. Bellman, *Marjorie Kinnan Rawlings,* p. 65.

29. Quoted in Tarr, *Max and Marjorie,* p. 116.

30. Quoted in Tarr, *Max and Marjorie,* p. 127.

31. Quoted in Tarr, *Max and Marjorie,* p. 129.

32. Quoted in Tarr, *Max and Marjorie,* p. 230.

33. Quoted in Tarr, *Max and Marjorie,* p. 233.

34. Quoted in Bellman, *Marjorie Kinnan Rawlings,* p. 70.

35. Marjorie Kinnan Rawlings, *The Yearling.* New York: Charles Scribner's Sons, 1966, p. 423.

36. Bigelow, *Frontier Eden,* pp. 79–80.

37. Michael Gannon, ed., *The New History of Florida.* Gainesville: University Press of Florida, 1996, p. 257.

38. Quoted in Tarr, *Max and Marjorie*, p. 257.

39. Quoted in Tarr, *Max and Marjorie*, p. 298.

40. Quoted in Tarr, *Max and Marjorie*, p. 308.

41. Bigelow, *Frontier Eden*, p. 134.

42. Walton, "A Novel of Backwoods Living," p. 2.

43. Soskin, "A Tom Sawyer of the Florida Scrub Lands," p. 1.

44. Bigelow, *Frontier Eden*, p. 136.

45. Walton, "A Novel of Backwoods Living," p. 2.

46. *Time*, "Books," April 4, 1938, p. 69.

Chapter 3: The Plot

47. Rawlings, *The Yearling*, p. 19.

48. Rawlings, *The Yearling*, p. 3.

49. Rawlings, *The Yearling*, p. 10.

50. Rawlings, *The Yearling*, p. 26.

51. Rawlings, *The Yearling*, p. 34.

52. Rawlings, *The Yearling*, p. 68.

53. Rawlings, *The Yearling*, p. 108.

54. Rawlings, *The Yearling*, p. 128.

55. Rawlings, *The Yearling*, pp. 129–30.

56. Rawlings, *The Yearling*, p. 158.

57. Rawlings, *The Yearling*, pp. 203–204.

58. Rawlings, *The Yearling*, p. 208.

59. Rawlings, *The Yearling*, p. 332.

60. Rawlings, *The Yearling*, p. 426.

Chapter 4: The Characters

61. Rawlings, *The Yearling*, p. 18.

62. Rawlings, *The Yearling*, p. 18.

63. Rawlings, *The Yearling*, p. 20.

64. Rawlings, *The Yearling*, p. 207.

65. Rawlings, *The Yearling*, p. 18.

66. Bellman, *Marjorie Kinnan Rawlings,* p. 74.

67. Rawlings, *The Yearling,* p. 206.

68. Rawlings, *The Yearling,* p. 301.

69. Rawlings, *The Yearling,* p. 186.

70. Rawlings, *The Yearling,* p. 299.

71. Rawlings, *The Yearling,* pp. 113–14.

72. Rawlings, *The Yearling,* p. 109.

Chapter 5: Literary Criticism

73. Lucille W. Van Vliet, *Approaches to Literature Through Genre.* Phoenix, AZ: Oryx Press, 1992, p. 184.

74. M. H. Abrams, *Glossary of Literary Terms.* Fort Worth, TX: Harcourt Brace Jovanovich, 1993, p. 174.

75. Soskin, "A Tom Sawyer of the Florida Scrub Lands," p. 1.

76. Walton, "A Novel of Backwoods Living," p. 2.

77. Bigelow, *Frontier Eden,* p. 152.

78. "Books," p. 69.

79. Marjorie Kinnan Rawlings, "Regional Literature of the South," *College English,* February 1940, pp. 381, 385.

80. Bigelow, *Frontier Eden,* p. 70.

81. Rawlings, *The Yearling,* p. 95.

82. Gordon E. Bigelow, "Marjorie Kinnan Rawlings' Wilderness," *Sewanee Review,* Spring 1965, p. 305.

83. Lamar York, "Marjorie Kinnan Rawlings's Rivers," *Southern Literary Journal,* Spring 1977, pp. 92, 103.

84. Daniels, "Boy in the Backwoods," p. 5.

85. Stuckey, *The Pulitzer Prize Novels,* p. 117.

86. *Atlantic Monthly,* "The Atlantic Bookshelf: A Guide to Good Books," June 1938.

87. Bellman, *Marjorie Kinnan Rawlings,* p. 73.

88. Stuckey, *The Pulitzer Prize Novels,* p. 117.

89. Soskin, "A Tom Sawyer of the Florida Scrub Lands," p. 1.

90. Bellman, *Marjorie Kinnan Rawlings,* p. 54.

91. Soskin, "A Tom Sawyer of the Florida Scrub Lands," p. 2.

92. Bigelow, *Frontier Eden,* pp. 150, 151.

93. Silverthorne, *Marjorie Kinnan Rawlings,* p. 142.

94. Samuel I. Bellman, "Marjorie Kinnan Rawlings: A Solitary Sojourner in the Florida Backwoods," *Kansas Quarterly,* Spring 1970, p. 82.

95. McDonnell, "A Second Look: *The Yearling,*" p. 345.

96. Rawlings, *The Yearling,* p. 426.

97. McDonnell, "A Second Look: *The Yearling,*" p. 344.

98. Walton, "A Novel of Backwoods Living," p. 2.

99. Soskin, "A Tom Sawyer of the Florida Scrub Lands," p. 2.

100. Rawlings, *The Yearling,* p. 428.

101. Stuckey, *The Pulitzer Prize Novels,* p. 116.

For Further Exploration

1. Critics such as W. J. Stuckey argue that *The Yearling* is sentimental, sappy, and not deserving of serious critical attention. On the other hand, Samuel I. Bellman insists that some serious readers are misled by the book's "surface sentimentality" and that the story's message is actually one of a frightened and lost child who is crying out in despair. With whom do you agree? Choose incidents from the book to support your decision. *See also*: Samuel I. Bellman, *Marjorie Kinnan Rawlings*; W. J. Stuckey, *The Pulitzer Prize Novels: A Critical Backward Look*.

2. Marjorie Kinnan Rawlings stated that she used Penny as a vehicle to express her philosophy of life. Find incidents in which Penny reveals his philosophy of life and explain what ideas he is conveying through his words and actions. *See also*: Samuel I. Bellman, "Marjorie Kinnan Rawlings: A Solitary Sojourner in the Florida Backwoods."

3. John Steinbeck's *The Red Pony* is also a story about a boy named Jody who has a pet that dies. According to Samuel I. Bellman, *The Red Pony* greatly influenced Rawlings and, therefore, *The Yearling*. Read *The Red Pony* and discuss the similarities and differences between the stories. Do the books have the same overall message? Why or why not? *See also*: John Steinbeck, *The Red Pony*; Samuel I. Bellman, *Marjorie Kinnan Rawlings*.

4. The St. Johns River appears frequently throughout *The Yearling*. Consider how the river is described, what it does, and what occurs on the river. Use this knowledge to describe the river's symbolic meaning in the novel. *See also*: Lamar York, "Marjorie Kinnan Rawlings's Rivers."

5. Choose two incidents from the book, one in which the wilderness is a place of beauty or comfort and another in which the wilderness is a place of danger. Use these two different incidents to examine the "wilderness" of *The Yearling* and discuss its overall characteristics in the book. *See also*: Gordon E. Bigelow, "Marjorie Kinnan Rawlings' Wilderness."

6. Critics argue that there is a symbolic relationship between Jody and Flag. For instance, when Flag is dead, Jody feels as though his childhood has died with him. Choose at least three incidents in the book that include both Jody and Flag. Discuss the similarities and differences in their actions and/or states of being. *See also*: Edith H. Walton, "A Novel of Backwoods Living"; William

Soskin, "A Tom Sawyer of the Florida Scrub Lands"; W. J. Stuckey, *The Pulitzer Prize Novels: A Critical Backward Look.*

7. Locate passages in the book that you believe support Marjorie Kinnan Rawlings's doctrine that every person must find the particular environment in which he or she can achieve the greatest happiness. Explain how you think these passages support that belief. *See also*: Gordon E. Bigelow, "Marjorie Kinnan Rawlings' Wilderness"; Marjorie Kinnan Rawlings, *Cross Creek.*

8. When Jody meets Nellie Ginright, he decides that women run "in breeds" and Nellie was of Grandma Hutto's breed. Use examples to explain the different "breeds" of women Marjorie Kinnan Rawlings presents in *The Yearling*. *See also*: Samuel I. Bellman, *Marjorie Kinnan Rawlings.*

9. What do you like about Jody Baxter? Use passages from the text to explain Jody's personality and the things that make readers like him. Compare your reasons to those put forth by Samuel I. Bellman and/or William Soskin. *See also*: Samuel I. Bellman, *Marjorie Kinnan Rawlings*; William Soskin, "A Tom Sawyer of the Florida Scrub Lands."

Appendix of Criticism

An Adolescent Classic

The Yearling tells the story of one year in the life of a tow-headed, lively 12-year-old named Jody Baxter. The Baxter clearing is even more remote than that of most crackers, but in his own eyes Jody lives an eventful life. There is no school within reach. His days are spent mostly roaming the game-filled woods, hunting bear and deer with his kindhearted pa and a clan of big, bearded, hell-raising moonshiners and horse traders. Occasionally his pa takes him to visit a hearty old woman who lives in a village on the St. Johns River. He sees a flood, afterward goes hunting where stranded wild animals are thicker than flies. Jody's pal is a pet fawn. He takes it on hunting trips, even sleeps with it when he can get around his fussy, practical ma. The idyl [*sic*] ends when hard scrub reality forces him to kill his fawn because it cannot be kept out of the corn patch.

With its excellent descriptions of Florida scrub landscapes, its skillful use of native vernacular, its tender relations between Jody and his pet fawn, *The Yearling* is a simply written, picturesque story of boyhood that stands a good chance, when adults have finished with it, of finding a permanent place in adolescent libraries.

Time, "Books," April 4, 1938.

Jody Is the Most Charming Boy in American Fiction

With Tom Sawyer, Huckleberry Finn and the lesser members of the fraternity of young boys in American literature well in mind, it is quite possible to maintain that Jody Baxter, son of the farmer and huntsman, Penny Baxter, in Marjorie Kinnan Rawlings' new novel, "The Yearling," is the most charming boy in the entire national gallery. He may lack some of the sense of mischief and the adolescent wryness which have endeared Mark Twain's kids to our hearts. But Jody, roaming in the scrub forests of Mrs. Rawlings' favorite Florida country, living close to his animals with a sensitive emotional understanding of them, learning the subtleties of life which a child in sophisticated communities can never know, and reflecting that wholesomeness in his own spirit, has a gayety and a bubbling humor which run far deeper than that of any of the famous adolescents of our literature.

Out of [the] landscape of life in the Florida scrub, woven closely with unforgettable portraits of native people in their kitchens, in their churches, in ceremonies of birth and death, in their tragedies and their virile battles against the elements, Mrs. Rawlings draws a story with a tragic climax—that of the end of youth. It is because we have known the innermost recesses of Jody's heart and the intimacy of his dreams that the ultimate need to kill the fawn becomes a drama of overpowering proportions. It is written with a thorough poignance, and yet with a fine sense of detachment and of the normal flow of life that leavens all such tragedies of youth. As a result of the death of the fawn young Jody comes eventually to know that his yearling days are over, as are his pet's.

William Soskin, "A Tom Sawyer of the
Florida Scrub Lands: Introducing the Most Charming
Boy in Our National Gallery,"
New York Herald Tribune Books, April 3, 1938.

The Story of Jody's Coming of Age Is the Best Thing Rawlings Has Written

Already published by Marjorie Kinnan Rawlings are two novels and innumerable short stories about the isolated, backwoods people who live in the wild heart of the far-flung Florida scrub. Her name is identified with the region. . . . For all that and despite her previous accomplishments, Mrs. Rawlings has written nothing even comparable in excellence to "The Yearling." A feeble plot, superimposed arbitrarily, was the weakness of "South Moon Under" and especially of "Golden Apples." In "The Yearling," however—which is merely a simple chronicle of the life of one significant year in the life of a 12-year-old boy—Mrs. Rawlings has not allowed herself to be hampered by plot requirements. Character and background are her sole consideration; in a narrative of moving beauty she has achieved complete integration between them. . . .

The story catches one up into the rhythm of wilderness living. Its crises become as important as they were to Penny and Jody. The pursuit of old Slewfoot, the vicious, thieving bear; the great storm, with its aftermath of flood and pestilence; the attack of famished wolves upon the Baxters' enclosure; the occasional, exciting trips to Volusia, the river town—out of such simple episodes as these Mrs. Rawlings has fashioned a tale which in effect is remarkably dramatic. As well, there is the spicy recurring comedy of the Baxters' relations with the Forresters—who are at one moment kindly neighbors, at another lawless brutes. . . .

Certain virtues one expects from Mrs. Rawlings. She has, for example, a marvelous ear for the flavorsome cracker dialect, she makes one see and smell the lonely arid scrub. Never before, however, has she created a set of characters who are so close and real to the reader, whose intimate life one can share without taint of unconscious patronage. In most books of this kind, including the author's own, the backwoods folk of the South are distressingly quaint and alien. They belong, seemingly, to a different race, a different world. Penny and Jody how ever, for all their lack of schooling, have a natural, sensitive intelligence which one respects and responds to from the start. They are people of worth and dignity, inarticulate but wise. "The Yearling"—and this is the best tribute one can pay it—is nothing so narrowly limited as a "local-color" novel. Rather, it casts with unusual beauty the old, timeless story of youth's growth to maturity.

> Edith H. Walton, "A Novel of Backwoods Living:
> Marjorie Kinnan Rawlings Writes with Unusual
> Beauty a Story of Youth's Growth to Maturity," *New
> York Times Book Review,* April 3, 1938.

Sometimes Sentimental, but Wise and Moving as Well

There comes a moment everywhere when ceasing to be a boy may be a tragedy like dying. But the story of that moment has never been more tenderly written than by Marjorie Kinnan Rawlings in this novel of Jody, one boy of the Florida hammock country, and Flag, the faun [*sic*], who grew together out of a frolicking youngness to the bitter qualities of maturity. . . .

Mrs. Rawlings had written a wise and moving book informed with a love of all living kind. It falters occasionally into sentimentality. When she writes of the town beyond the scrub, of lavender scented Grandma Hutto and her sailor son Oliver who loved the yellow-haired girl—whom Lem Forrester did not mean he should have without a murderous mauling—the book sometimes seems artificial and shaped for trivial story. But in the wilderness, on the hunt, in the storm, in the face of impending hunger and encircling jungle, her people are real and living. Certainly they are never mere bush beaters for local color. Isolated, they are not remote. As Mrs. Rawlings writes we are all there in the scrub; and beyond the sanctuary of boyhood and the security of clearing, struggle and burden, fear and weariness await us all.

Jonathan Daniels, "Boy in the Backwoods,"
Saturday Review of Literature, April 2, 1938.

Child Characters in Adult Fiction: A Tricky Business

Writing fiction for adults about a child in a child's world is a delicately difficult literary undertaking. Too many writers attempt it. Most of them fail. Perhaps a major reason for the failures is that most such stories either are frankly autobiographical or become so despite the author's desperate struggles. Leaning wistfully back into the mind and person of the child he thinks he was, the writer produces a character made up of his own hurts and nostalgias, of impossibly mature and knowing afterthoughts, of his sad desire to think that, had not life so strangely buffeted him, he would have been all the great and beautiful things his infant self must surely of [*sic*] contained. The results are usually garbled amateur psychiatric tracts, and very rarely literature.

Marjorie Kinnan Rawlings has succeeded where so many others have failed, and *The Yearling* is a distinguished book. . . .

Even a [Henry David] Thoreau cannot report on the world outdoors as a child might. The naturalist sees only those things which concern his informed eyes. To a child the barn and the woodshed are as much a part of the natural workable landscape as the lizard under the log. Mrs. Rawlings has done a small miracle in that she knows this, never stops to interpret, never once steps outside Jody's perceptions, never mars her great skill by pausing to explain. She has captured a child's time sense, in which everything lasts forever and the change of season takes him always unawares.

Atlantic Monthly, "The Atlantic Bookshelf: A
Guide to Good Books," June 1938.

Marjorie Kinnan Rawlings's Scrub and Storms

The primordial wilderness of the scrub had a strong appeal for [Marjorie Kinnan Rawlings]; she liked the notion that there never had been human habitation in the scrub and probably never would be, that she might cross where no man had ever crossed before. Because the soil was dry and sandy, there had been little to attract pioneer farmers into the area during the nineteenth century when other parts of central Florida were being settled; and after the big cypress had been cut from along the Oklawaha River, there was little to attract capitalists, so that when Marjorie first knew the scrub in the early 1930's, hardly more than half a dozen families lived in it except for small settlements along the Oklawaha and at Lake Kerr. It had remained literally a frontier area where a man could still make a living with an axe and a gun.

In her passion for authenticity she acquired extensive knowledge of the history of the scrub and used accurately a number of historical references in her stories. The devastating northeaster which blew for nearly a week in 1871 and flooded many parts of the scrub became a central event in *The Yearling*.

Gordon E. Bigelow, *Frontier Eden: The Literary Career of Marjorie Kinnan Rawlings*. Gainesville: University of Florida Press, 1966.

Life on the St. Johns River in 1870s Florida

Soon [after the Civil War] magazines, newspapers, and railroad companies were sending reporters to observe and report on this paradise. By 1870 Floridians were publishing the *Florida New Yorker* to attract settlers and investors. Jacksonville, which had been almost destroyed by the frequent invasions of the war years, bounced back to become the center of winter tourism, the gateway to southern Florida via the St. Johns River, and a budding financial center where northern capital was increasingly available for investment. Hubbard Hart's line of steamers was one of several which carried passengers and freight up the St. Johns. . . .

Frederick DeBary, a Belgian wine merchant, also transported visitors up the St. Johns as far as Lake Monroe, where he built a hotel at the new community named for him. The Brock Line operated between Jacksonville and Enterprise on the northern shore of Lake Monroe. Small shallow-draft steamers plied the torturous channels of the upper St. Johns with passengers and cargo bound for the Indian River settlements of Titusville, Rockledge, and Eau Gallie. With three large hotels, Rockledge soon became known as the southernmost winter resort in the nation.

Jerrell H. Shofner, "Reconstruction and Renewal, 1865–1877," in Michael Gannon, ed., *The New History of Florida*. Gainesville: University Press of Florida, 1996.

89

The Yearling Is Amateurish, Slight, and Sentimental

In 1939, the Pulitzer jury again by-passed the best serious fiction of the year ([William] Faulkner's *Unvanquished,* and Allen Tate's *The Fathers*) and selected the year's biggest best seller, Marjorie Kinnan Rawlings' *The Yearling.* The desire to get on the band wagon of a "big" winner was, again, not the only factor operating in this decision. *The Yearling* has many of the tested and true Pulitzer ingredients to recommend it. It is "local history" of pioneer life on the Florida frontier just after the Civil War, and like *The Able McLaughlins* and *Lamb in His Bosom,* it is packed with homely detail about the lives of rude, backwoods people and their houses, husbandry, and speech. Interwoven with these picturesque details is the sentimental story of a boy named Jody who finds a new-born deer, domesticates it, dotes upon it, and finally allows his mother to destroy it for trampling down the family's crops. In a rather amateurish attempt to give her story implications larger than it can bear, Mrs. Rawlings, at the close of the book, tries to make the death of the yearling deer symbolic of the end of Jody's boyhood: "Somewhere beyond the sink-hole, past the magnolia, under the live oaks, a boy and a yearling ran side by side and were gone forever." . . .

[*The Yearling*] is . . . too slight and sentimental to merit serious attention. Mrs. Rawlings' writing is generally amateurish. Her style owes much to [Ernest] Hemingway, but lacks Hemingway's precision and coherence of effect. Such artistic defects, of course, are not likely to bother the unsophisticated readers [at] whom the book seems, consciously or unconsciously, aimed. One can well imagine that, unlike many Pulitzer novels, *The Yearling* will over the years continue to attract young readers.

> W. J. Stuckey, *The Pulitzer Prize Novels: A Critical Backward Look*. Norman: University of Oklahoma Press, 1966.

The Yearling, a Nightmare Story

Mrs. Rawlings describes a nightmare world where things continue to go wrong, and where the noblest resolve, the loftiest intention, and the most arduous toil are quite unavailing. Again and again, for all the surface sentimentality that has misled serious readers, the story echoes a frightened and lost child crying in the night, out of fear, disappointment, and despair. . . . It is best to examine [Rawlings's] dark, brooding drama through an analysis of the three protagonists—Ma Baxter, her husband Penny, and their son Jody.

Ma Baxter is a bitter, complaining woman who has little patience with anyone. . . . Jody grows up father- and male-oriented, and his mother is a kind of stereotyped female ogre like the widows and aunts in *Tom Sawyer* and *Huckleberry Finn: She just won't let a boy have no fun nohow.* Most of the time, she gives Jody (and Penny too) "the miseries," and so the reader is tempted to write her off as a sorry example of a mother and wife. . . .

It is not hard to understand why [Ma] was so unpleasant and formidable a person, or why she infused gloom and unhappiness into Jody's thirteenth year, just when the world was opening up to him. . . . She had been deprived, for a long time, of the opportunity for maternal expression. Even after Ma's great need had somehow been satisfied to an extent, force of habit (or an emotional lag—what I am tempted to call "emotional hysteresias") made her continue to project the customary baleful influence on those around her. It was almost as though she were lost between two worlds: the realm of *should have been* and the realm of *came too late.* Thus, in the light of the clearly developed picture we have of Jody's mother, the curt remark by the author—"Her good nature rose and fell with the food supply"—cannot possibly be taken at face value. But the haunting aftereffects of a lost family constitute only part of the nightmare story that comprises *The Yearling.* . . .

Penny is a man who has been severely injured by life—aside from the deaths of all the Baxter children who preceded Jody, his difficulties with his wife, and the snake-bite and the rupture that lay him low in the course of the story. His childhood, in a large farm family living near a village some distance from the Big Scrub, was characterized by adverse conditions: unremitting toil, short rations, and hookworm. His own father had been an austere preacher, and Penny's social growth was as severely stunted as his physical devel opment. From this derived his trauma, which Mrs. Rawlings com ments on vaguely but provocatively.

Penny could not stand the press of people around him. . . . What lies behind this morbid sensitivity to social encroachment on the part of Penny? . . . Given our present state of knowledge, it is enough for our purposes merely to think that a deeper explanation exists for Penny's attitude . . . than simple touchiness or cantankerousness.

Lastly, there is twelve-year-old Jody, growing up in isolation and molded by his father's morbid hypersensitivity to overcrowding and his mother's pervasive bitter pessimism. But Jody emerges at the beginning of the story not as a neurotic, anti-social, emotional cripple, but as a wholesome country boy who is enormously excited by the renewed promise and glory of a North Florida April. The sensitive reader of any age and background cannot help but share Jody's delight in his woolgathering rambles and hunting and fishing trips, his worry over the calamities that befall his father, his fear over the threats to his family's food supply, and, finally, his ordeal in having to kill Flag, which had become a part of him and in effect a member of the family. . . .

The alienation, confusion, anxiety, and time-sensitivity that underlie the novel are most sharply focused at the end with Jody's killing of Flag. Why should life have to be this way? Well, it just is. Jody did not believe he would ever love anybody again as he had Flag.

Samuel I. Bellman, *Marjorie Kinnan Rawlings.*
New York: Twayne, 1974.

The Symbolism of the St. Johns River

Rawlings uses rivers in her writings as the chief aspect of place and as the chief thematic element of setting. In all her stories in which man seeks to identify with his natural environment, there is a consciousness of the river either as the outside limits of the setting or as the connecting link between her setting and the rest of the world. . . .

In . . . *The Yearling,* the river occupies less of Rawlings's attention, but it is as instrumental here in helping the characters find a sense of place as it was in any of the previous stories. The St. Johns River is the instrument of the young hero Jody's *rite de passage* [rite of passage] from yearling to manhood.

The river does not appear in the novel till midway, when Jody and his father Penny go out from their scrub homestead to the fringe of civilization lining the banks of the river—emphasizing again Marjorie Rawlings's use of rivers as the outer edge of her microcosmic scrub. She reminds the reader of the river's great importance to all life and commerce. She brings it to life as a "deep and placid river, alive with craft, with dug outs and scows, lumber rafts, and freight passenger vessels, side-wheel steamers that almost filled the stream, in places, from bank to bank. . . ." Before it enters prominently into the life of Jody or Penny, however, the river already has a character all its own: "The river flowed deep and dark.

It made a rippling sound against the banks, but the great liquid heart of it moved silently." Its "watery tentacles held him" when Jody tried to learn to swim it. The river permeates life at Volusia, the river settlement where Jody and his father Penny have gone to visit Grandma Hutto; there "lay the smell of the river. The river itself was fluid through the cottage and around it, leaving a whirlpool of odorousness and dampness and decaying fern."

But the boy Jody senses the river's greatness even before it becomes the instrument of his self-discovery. He recognizes its character when he first sees it, though he cannot yet know the dramatic role the river will play in his own life. The St. Johns that Penny and Jody see as they arrive at Volusia "was dark, and aloof. It seemed to slide toward the ocean indifferent to its own banks and to the men who crossed it or used it. Jody stared at it. It was a pathway to the world."

Jody does not yet understand the river's significance to his discovery of a "sense of place" even when he sees it clearly as the pathway on which his beloved friends Grandma and Oliver Hutto are carried out of his life. But his perception of the river in that episode is the motivation for his return to the river for help when the time comes that he must find his own identity.

This episode, which is Mrs. Rawlings's most poignant and dramatic use of the river in *The Yearling,* and perhaps anywhere in her fiction, appears in the closing pages of Jody's story. As countless readers and moviegoers will remember, he has been required to kill his pet deer, Flag, in order to prevent it from eating the tender young corn crop that would see the family and the stock through the winter. Killing the pet he adores is the most painful ordeal he has ever undergone, and it is altogether natural for him, after concluding that he must leave home, that he then "better get on the river itself at once." Initially, his plan is to go to Oliver and Grandma Hutto, now in Boston, and the river responds as a great magnet: "The wind behind him helped him, and it seemed to him that he could feel the northbound current of the great river." But now without the sense of place he had in the scrub, he is soon lost: ". . . [He] headed for the open water. He was out in the world, and it seemed to him that he was alien here, and alone, and then he was being carried away into a void." Alone on the river, he comes to understand what everyone must: the self he discovers is not a new one but the old self that had been awaiting discovery. But dissociation from the scrub home he knew so well has forced on him the consciousness that he will not find himself by getting away from the scrub. Life is a mystery anywhere, he discovers, as "Darkness filled both land and water," but he is now ready to move toward reconciliation with himself and with the place that he once called home. He is at his nadir, between his old childlike acceptance of life as a sure thing and his coming reconciliation with his adult role in the scrub homestead. He is, during the time he spends on the river, in that place between childhood and manhood, "suspended in a timeless place. He could go neither forwards nor back. Something was ended. Nothing was begun." But he has made the break with his own former acceptance of life as an exclusively good and happy thing: "he had been out in the world, and the world was a troubled dream, fluid and desolate, flanked by swamps and cypresses."

Jody is rescued from the river by the government mail boat and returned to the river settlement at Volusia where, symbolically, he is put ashore on the east bank, and so must cross the river once more to make his way to Baxter's Island and home. As he comes to the top knoll on the long walk home, he can look back at the lake and the river he had thought to use as his escape. It has been the instrument of his new understanding, and has actually participated beneficently in his growing up: "It was pitilessly blue. Thin white lines were the implacable choppy waves that had turned him back to the unfriendly shore." He passes the pathway leading down to the tiny crystal clear stream where he was seen daydreaming on the book's opening page. He wants to return now to that happy place. . . . But it is not the same place he remembers, any more than he is the person he was on the beginning page. Jody sees that he already has made the trip on that tiny stream of his childhood as far as it can take him; he has begun the journey now on an infinitely larger stream. When he looked at this stream a year ago, he was filled with childhood excitement. . . . The river has taught him maturity; again the river encloses that universe which all of Marjorie Rawlings's characters inhabit.

Lamar York, "Marjorie Kinnan Rawlings's Rivers,"
Southern Literary Journal, Spring 1977.

The Wilderness in Rawlings's Works

Throughout [Rawlings's] writings the wilderness theme is closely associated with a developed doctrine concerning the relation of man to his environment. She believed, briefly, that a man can be happy only in the degree to which he is able to adjust harmoniously to his surroundings. The more natural those surroundings, and the more completely he is in harmony with them, the greater will be his happiness. . . .

On one side Mrs. Rawlings was a true romantic in her treatment of nature and the frontier, stressing strangeness, uniqueness, and the distance of a nostalgically conceived past. . . .

But on another side she was a thoroughgoing realist. "I know you think I put too much emphasis on the importance of fact in fiction," she wrote [Max] Perkins after *The Yearling* was published, "but it seems to me that this type of work is not valid if the nature lore behind it is not true in every detail." Because she wished to tell the whole truth, the nature she depicts has not only idyllic beauty, as in the episode where Jody Baxter makes his fluttermill at Silver Glen Springs; it also has terror, as when Penny is struck by the rattlesnake, and an inscrutable cruelty, as when the great storm destroys the Baxter's [sic] crops and floods the scrub country so that the wild creatures are drowned by hundreds. . . .

[Rawlings's wilderness] is a jungle with most of its fangs drawn; the predators—wolf, bear, or aborigine—have either been eliminated or are being rapidly destroyed, so as to leave predominantly a wilderness of flora, along with the comfortable lesser fauna to give one the thrill of encounter with the brute. . . . Hers is also a wilderness which contains or borders upon plowed fields, and her attitudes toward wild nature are almost inextricably enmeshed with agrarian attitudes, and both of these come from an essentially mystic insistence upon a holy harmony between man and earth, between man and the life of the cosmos. Both of these are parts of a protest against the "strange disease of modern life," and a plea for a return to simpler, more natural ways. The extraordinary beauty of her wilderness she conveys in a language of extraordinary beauty, a gift to her readers of which one could predict that the wilderness which can heal them is to be found less and less in nature and more and more in books like hers.

> Gordon E. Bigelow, "Marjorie Kinnan Rawlings'
> Wilderness," *Sewanee Review,* Spring 1965.

Rawlings's "Brushed Clean" Realism

Robert Frost spoke of two kinds of realist in literature, the one who offers a good deal of dirt with his potato to show it is a real potato, and the one who is satisfied with the potato brushed clean. Marjorie was a realist of the second kind, but one should add that her brushing-clean often included a considerable editing of the reality she presented. She reminds one in this respect of the American genre painters of the [nineteenth] century . . . who painted scenes from actual life, especially rural scenes, with a smooth, brightly lighted realism, but a cleaned-up realism which omitted the sordid and most forms of the ugly, gave a uniform pleasantry to their human subjects, and cast over the whole a nostalgia for a simpler, happier time now receded into the past. The reality which Marjorie depicts is much like this, particularly in the period pieces like *The Yearling,* except that there is less cheeriness because she also adds a considerable mixture of the darker tones of human anguish. Reading the book, one has the sense of experiencing a full life until he begins to enumerate the areas of experience which are omitted: most forms of human depravity and violence; virtually all sexual experience; almost all forms of social intercourse; the entire realms of politics, education, religion, and other forms of institutional life; except at a remote distance, there is in the book no nation, no state, and no city. She has deliberately restricted the subject . . . to a pastoral microcosm, a family living in a garden surrounded by the wilderness. Her entire focus is upon their elemental struggle to survive, and upon the elemental processes of human growth and decay. A boy, and his relation of love to his father, to the animal world and the world of nature; a father, with his patient fostering love for his child, his courage and great skill in providing for his family; the pain of irretrievable loss and of alienation from loved ones; the joy of reconciliation. No subject matter could be more universal, and none more fraught with peril of the obvious or the sentimental. This is the "what oft was thought" of the classicist, and because of the unrelenting discipline through which she gave it needed chastity and rigor, one is tempted to add, "ne'er so well express'd."

Gordon E. Bigelow, *Frontier Eden: The Literary Career of Marjorie Kinnan Rawlings.* Gainesville: University of Florida Press, 1966.

Penny's Philosophy

Penny Baxter will be remembered as the puny-sized hard-working farmer of the scrub country during the 1870s. Everything he says is particularly pithy and to the point: his funeral sermon at the grave of the crippled Forrester boy, Fodder-wing, is probably the finest piece of writing Mrs. Rawlings ever produced. A preacher manqué, this uncommonly good and wise man is practically always kind to all, and particularly patient with his ill-tempered, embittered wife. . . .

Mrs. Rawlings regarded Penny Baxter as her favorite character in *The Yearling,* because as she put it, through him she expressed her philosophy of life. Thus it was not only Penny's profound attachment to his only son Jody that linked him with Mrs. Rawlings, who had always harbored a tender feeling for little boys, and deeply regretted her childlessness. It was also the fact that he was the perfect vehicle, with his patient wisdom through protracted adversity, for her own creed of stoic acceptance of life's slings and arrows. At the end of the story Penny is severely incapacitated as a result of rupturing himself while working in the field. He had been forced to order his wife to shoot Jody's yearling deer, which had grown too big for the impoverished Baxter family to support, and the outraged Jody, after berating his bed-ridden father with a vehement malediction, ran away from home. Not long after, he returns, and Penny is overjoyed that he has his beloved son back, after all the miseries they have been through. It's food and drink to have Jody home [Jody's presence sustains his father spiritually just as food and drink sustain him physically.] Penny tells Jody what he thinks life is all about:

> "You've seed how things goes in the world o' men. You've knowed men to be low-down and mean. You've seed ol' Death at his tricks. You've messed around with ol' Starvation. Ever' man wants life to be a fine thing, and a easy. 'Tis fine, boy, powerful fine, but 'tain't easy. Life knocks you down agin. I've been uneasy all my life. . . . I've wanted life to be easy for you. Easier'n 'twas for me. A man's heart aches, seein' his young uns face the world. Knowin' they got to git their guts tore out, the way his was tore. I wanted to spare you, long as I could. I wanted you to frolic with your yearlin'. I knowed the lonesomeness he eased for you. But ever' man's lonesome. What's he to do then? What's he to do when he gits knocked down? Why, take it for his share and go on."

Samuel I. Bellman, "Marjorie Kinnan Rawlings:
A Solitary Sojourner in the Florida Backwoods,"
Kansas Quarterly, Spring 1970.

The Philosophy of The Yearling

You probably remember *The Yearling,* the story of Jody Baxter and his fawn Flag, how Jody raised Flag, and Flag followed him everywhere; Jody loved Flag more than anything, but Flag grew up and finally had to be killed to keep him from destroying the family crops. That is what I remember from my childhood reading. I cried over it, much the same way I cried over *Black Beauty, Lassie Come Home,* and *Old Yeller. The Yearling* is a tear-jerker, with lots of action: hunting, fighting, natural disasters. But as an adult reader, these are not the ingredients that interest me. Instead, I am fascinated, shocked actually, by the view of life that Marjorie Kinnan Rawlings reveals in this story, a view so strong, bleak, but reassuring, that I am surprised to find it in a book that has deeply affected so many children. Her adult characters are varied, fallible and, most intriguing to me, they are vulnerable. The life they are caught in is unpredictable and relentlessly hard. And the attitude they take toward it is totally without delusions, but powerful in its compassion and in its determination to survive.

The clearest example of this attitude is Penny Baxter, Jody's father. . . . Penny has settled in the rough Florida scrub, away from civilized towns. . . .

Penny had hoped to fill his island with children, but one after the other his babies die in infancy. Finally, Jody is born. Penny rejoices in him, but suffers as he sees Jody feel life's pain. . . .

Penny is a man of absolute honesty and deep compassion. He accepts the differences in people, their strengths and weaknesses alike. He sees the universality in suffering. . . .

Penny is Marjorie Rawlings' spokesman in the story. His fathering of Jody is rich and reliable. Instead of shielding or holding back, Penny comforts, commiserates, and reassures but never tries to deceive, never portrays life as anything other than the demanding experience that it is. Just as Penny's words comfort Jody and give him the strength to continue, so Rawlings' message excites and reassures me. How powerful it is to come to terms with the duality of life, the pain and the joy, and to learn to believe in your own strength and endurance, and how beautiful to realize the suffering of each man and to see it as something linked to your own.

Christine McDonnell, "A Second Look:
The Yearling," *Horn Book Magazine,* June 1977.

Animal Stories in Realistic Fiction

Stories about wild animals and birds as pets illustrate the perilous balance between animals and humans and the problems that can arise. Such stories include Marjorie Kinnan Rawling's [*sic*] *The Yearling*. . . .

In the realistic fiction genre, animals behave like animals. They are portrayed consistently and objectively. They are not given the power of speech or humanized. Characteristics and behavior of animals are realistically described. Some of the stories are based on true incidents or on the author's experiences with pets or wildlife. Incidents can be humorous, mysterious, adventurous, or sad. Conflicts are often animal against animal, animal against humans, or animals against society. The conflict can occur when an animal is mistreated, injured, or forced to change environments. Themes of love, responsibility, protection, human interaction, loyalty, and death are stressed in many realistic fiction stories.

Lucille W. Van Vliet, *Approaches to Literature Through Genre*. Phoenix, AZ: Oryx Press, 1992.

Chronology

1896
Marjorie Kinnan is born on August 8, in Washington, D.C., to Ida Traphagen Kinnan and Arthur Frank Kinnan, an examiner in the U.S. Patent Office.

1900
Rawlings's brother, Arthur Houston Kinnan, is born.

1907
Rawlings wins a $2 prize for a story that is published on the Sunday children's page of the *Washington Post*.

1912
Rawlings wins second prize in a *McCall's* contest for child authors. Her story is published and she receives $75.

1913
On January 31, Arthur Frank Kinnan dies of a kidney infection.

1914
In June, Rawlings graduates from Western High School in Washington, D.C. That summer, Austria declares war on Serbia, marking the beginning of the First World War. Also that summer, Ida moves the family to Madison, Wisconsin. In September, Rawlings enters the University of Wisconsin as an English major.

1917
The United States enters World War I, and many of the University of Wisconsin's male students leave school to fight the war.

1918
Rawlings graduates from the University of Wisconsin (Phi Beta Kappa in junior year) and moves to New York City, where she works as an editor for the National Board of the YWCA. In November, World War I ends.

1919
The Eighteenth Amendment outlawing the consumption, sale, and transportation of alcohol is ratified in January. In May, Marjorie marries Charles Rawlings.

1920–1922
The couple moves to Louisville, Kentucky, where Rawlings writes feature articles for the Louisville *Courier-Journal*.

1922–1928
Marjorie and Charles return to Rochester, where she writes features for two Rochester papers, the *Evening-Journal* and the *American*. In May 1926, she begins writing a daily syndicated feature, "Songs of a Housewife," which she continues to write until February 1928.

1928
In March, Marjorie and Charles take a trip to visit his brothers in Florida. They buy Cross Creek property later that summer and move to Florida in November; an inspired Rawlings immediately begins to make notes about the land and the people.

1929
The stock market crashes, catalyzing the Great Depression.

1930
Rawlings sells her first story, "Cracker Chidlings," to *Scribner's* in March for $150. She sells her second, "Jacob's Ladder," to them in December for $700. She becomes a protégé of *Scribner's* editor, Max Perkins.

1931
"Cracker Chidlings" is published in the February issue of *Scribner's,* followed by "Jacob's Ladder," which wins second prize in a *Scribner's* contest in April. Rawlings lives with the Fiddia family in the scrub from August to October to research her first novel.

1933
Rawlings's first novel, *South Moon Under,* is published in March and is an immediate success. She and Charles separate in March, and the divorce is final in November. Perkins suggests that she consider writing a "child's book of the scrub" (eventually *The Yearling*) in June. Rawlings does research for her next book by spending time living with Cal Long and his family in the scrub, and August to September on a trip to England. Receives a $500 O. Henry prize for "Gal Young 'Un." In December, Congress ratifies the Twenty-first Amendment making alcohol consumption legal again.

1934
Completes draft of second novel, *Golden Apples,* and sells condensed version to *Cosmopolitan.*

1935
Golden Apples is published. Rawlings breaks her neck falling from a horse.

1936
Rawlings meets Ernest Hemingway and F. Scott Fitzgerald through Perkins. Begins to write *The Yearling*.

1938
The Yearling is published in February. It becomes an instant best-seller and a Book-of-the-Month Club selection. The movie rights are sold. Rawlings gains national celebrity.

1939
Rawlings is awarded membership in the National Institute of Arts and Letters. She receives the Pulitzer Prize in fiction for *The Yearling*. In the fall, World War II begins as Germany invades Poland. Rawlings receives an honorary degree from Rollins College.

1940
A collection of Rawlings's short stories, *When the Whippoorwill*, is published. She begins writing *Cross Creek*.

1941
Rawlings completes *Cross Creek* and receives an honorary degree from the University of Florida. She marries Norton Baskin. The newlyweds purchase Castle Warden, a hotel in St. Augustine. Rawlings divides her time between St. Augustine and Cross Creek. In December, the United States enters World War II.

1942
In February, *Cross Creek* is published and becomes a best-seller. Later that year, Rawlings publishes a cookbook titled *Cross Creek Cookery*.

1943
Neighbor Zelma Cason files a $100,000 libel suit against Rawlings for the way that she was portrayed in *Cross Creek*. Rawlings begins work on *The Sojourner*. Norton Baskin goes off to war as an ambulance driver.

1944
Rawlings writes letters and corresponds with servicemen as part of the war effort. Late in the fall, Baskin returns home from the war quite ill.

1945
Rawlings continues work on *The Sojourner* and also publishes short fiction. She wins the O. Henry Memorial Award for "Black Secret." World War II ends.

1946

The libel—now considered "invasion of privacy"—case filed by Zelma Cason goes to trial. The decision is in Rawlings's favor, but Cason appeals and the case goes before the Florida Supreme Court. MGM releases *The Yearling* movie.

1947

The Florida Supreme Court decides in favor of Cason (4 – 3) and Rawlings is ordered to pay $1, plus Cason's legal fees. Maxwell Perkins dies. *Mountain Prelude,* a novella, is serialized by the *Saturday Evening Post.* Rawlings buys and renovates a farmhouse in Van Hornesville, New York.

1952

Rawlings has a coronary spasm in February while working on *The Sojourner.* She recovers and finally completes the book in August.

1953

The Sojourner is published in January. Rawlings begins research for a biography of Pulitzer Prize–winning author Ellen Glasgow. On December 14, Rawlings dies of a brain hemorrhage and is buried in Antioch Cemetery near Island Grove, Florida.

1955

A children's book, *The Secret River,* is published posthumously.

1956

The Secret River receives the Newbery Medal of Honor.

1963

The Yearling receives the Lewis Carroll Shelf Award.

Works Consulted

Major Editions of *The Yearling*

Marjorie Kinnan Rawlings (decorations by Edward Shenton), *The Yearling*. New York: Charles Scribner's Sons, 1938. This is the original publication.

———,(with pictures by N. C. Wyeth), *The Yearling*. New York: Charles Scribner's Sons, 1939. This edition includes full-page illustrations.

———,(with pictures by N. C. Wyeth), *The Yearling*. New York: Charles Scribner's Sons, 1940. This edition is considered the Pulitzer Prize edition.

———, *The Yearling*. New York: Council on Books in Wartime, 1943. This is the armed services edition.

———, (with decorations by Edward Shenton), *The Yearling*. New York: Charles Scribner's Sons, 1966. This is part of the Scribner's Library series (paperback).

———, (with pictures by N. C. Wyeth), *The Yearling*. New York: Atheneum, 1985. School and library bound edition.

———, *The Yearling: 50th Anniversary Edition*. New York: Macmillan, 1988. The fiftieth anniversary edition of the classic.

Letters and Additional Books of the Author

Gordon E. Bigelow and Laura V. Monti, eds., *Selected Letters of Marjorie Kinnan Rawlings*. Gainesville: University Presses of Florida, 1983. A collection of both personal and professional letters written by Marjorie Kinnan Rawlings.

Marjorie Kinnan Rawlings, *South Moon Under*. New York: Charles Scribner's Sons, 1933. Rawlings's first novel about a woman and her moonshining son in the scrub.

———, *Golden Apples*. New York: Charles Scribner's Sons, 1935. The story of an exiled Englishman who lives in the scrub and marries a native of that region.

———, *When the Whippoorwill*. New York: Charles Scribner's Sons, 1940. A collection of Rawlings's short stories.

———, "Regional Literature of the South," *College English*, February 1940.

————, *Cross Creek.* New York: Charles Scribner's Sons, 1942. Considered Rawlings's autobiography, *Cross Creek* sketches out a picture of her daily life at the creek.

————, *The Sojourner.* New York: Charles Scribner's Sons, 1953. The story of a midwestern farmer.

Rodger L. Tarr, *Short Stories by Marjorie Kinnan Rawlings.* Gainesville: University Press of Florida, 1994. A collection of Rawlings's short stories, with an introduction by Tarr.

————, *Songs of a Housewife: Poems by Marjorie Kinnan Rawlings.* Gainesville: University Press of Florida, 1997. A collection of the poems that Rawlings wrote for her syndicated column "Songs of a Housewife."

————, *Max and Marjorie: The Correspondence Between Maxwell E. Perkins and Marjorie Kinnan Rawlings.* Gainesville: University Press of Florida, 1999. This collection of letters between Marjorie and her editor and confidant Max Perkins provides insight into the day-to-day personality of Rawlings as well as the influence that Max Perkins had on her life and work.

John Hall Wheelock, *Editor to Author: The Letters of Maxwell E. Perkins.* New York: Charles Scribner's Sons, 1950. A collection of Perkins's letters to various authors, including Rawlings.

Biographical Information

Gordon E. Bigelow, *Frontier Eden: The Literary Career of Marjorie Kinnan Rawlings.* Gainesville: University of Florida Press, 1966. This is a very useful biography of Rawlings's literary career; it also contains literary criticism by the author.

Idella Parker, with Mary Keating, *Idella: Marjorie Kinnan Rawlings' "Perfect Maid."* Gainesville: University Press of Florida, 1992. Written by Parker, who worked as a "perfect maid" for Rawlings for almost thirteen years, this book provides the best account of Rawlings's actions and personality in her daily life.

Elizabeth Silverthorne, *Marjorie Kinnan Rawlings: Sojourner at Cross Creek.* Woodstock, NY: Overlook Press, 1988. The most complete biography of Rawlings to date.

Selected Reviews of *South Moon Under*

Herschel Brickell, "Florida Crackers in the Sandy Florida Scrub," *New York Herald Tribune Books,* March 5, 1933.

Jonathan Daniels, "Scrub Folk," *Saturday Review of Literature,* March 4, 1933.

Percy Hutchison, "Backwater Life in Florida's 'Scrub,'" *New York Times Book Review*, March 5, 1933.

Selected Reviews of *Golden Apples*

Henry Seidel Canby, "Wild Oranges," *Saturday Review of Literature*, October 5, 1935.

Percy Hutchison, "A Novel of the People in Florida's Swamps," *New York Times Book Review*, October 6, 1935.

Mary Ross, "When Pride Meets Pride," *New York Herald Tribune Books*, October 6, 1935.

Selected Reviews of *The Yearling*

Atlantic Monthly, "The Atlantic Bookshelf: A Guide to Good Books," June 1938.

Jonathan Daniels, "Boy in the Backwoods," *Saturday Review of Literature*, April 2, 1938.

William Soskin, "A Tom Sawyer of the Florida Scrub Lands," *New York Herald Tribune Books*, April 3, 1938.

Time, "Books," April 4, 1938.

Edith H. Walton, "A Novel of Backwoods Living," *New York Times Book Review*, April 3, 1938.

Selected Reviews of *When the Whippoorwill*

Atlantic Monthly, "The Atlantic Bookshelf," June 1940.

Rose Feld, "Stories That Warm the Heart," *New York Herald Tribune Books*, April 28, 1940.

Edith H. Walton, "Tales of the Florida Crackers," *New York Times Book Review*, April 28, 1940.

Selected Reviews of *Cross Creek*

Rose Feld, "Marjorie Rawlings and Her Neighbors," *New York Herald Tribune Books*, March 15, 1942.

Carroll Munro, "T'Other Side o' the Swamp," *Saturday Review of Literature*, April 4, 1942.

Katherine Woods, "In the Land of 'The Yearling,'" *New York Times Book Review*, March 15, 1942.

Selected Reviews of *The Sojourner*

Louis Bromfield, "Case of the Wandering Wits," *Saturday Review*, January 4, 1953.

Frances Gaither, "A World Compact and [original damaged]," *New York Times Book Review*, January 5, 1953.

Newsweek, "Rawlings Most Recent," January 5, 1953.

Coleman Rosenberger, "In This Luminous New Novel One Man's Story Is a Fable of Mankind," *Herald Tribune Book Review,* January 4, 1953.

Literary Criticism

M. H. Abrams, *Glossary of Literary Terms.* Fort Worth, TX: Harcourt Brace Jovanovich, 1993. Provides useful definitions of various literary terms including realism.

Samuel I. Bellman, *Marjorie Kinnan Rawlings.* New York: Twayne, 1974. This book contains fairly extensive criticism of the works of Marjorie Kinnan Rawlings, as well as a brief biographical sketch.

———, "Marjorie Kinnan Rawlings: A Solitary Sojourner in the Florida Backwoods," *Kansas Quarterly,* Spring 1970.

Gordon E. Bigelow, "Marjorie Kinnan Rawlings' Wilderness," *Sewanee Review,* Spring 1965.

Christine McDonnell, "A Second Look: *The Yearling,*" *Horn Book Magazine,* June 1977.

W. J. Stuckey, *The Pulitzer Prize Novels: A Critical Backward Look.* Norman: University of Oklahoma Press, 1966. Stuckey reexamines the Pulitzer Prize winners and identifies trends in selection. He is none too pleased with the selection of *The Yearling.*

Annette Trefzer, "Floating Homes and Signifiers in Hurston's and Rawlings's Autobiographies," *Southern Quarterly: A Journal of the Arts of the South,* Spring 1998.

Lucille W. Van Vliet, *Approaches to Literature Through Genre.* Phoenix, AZ: Oryx Press, 1992. An educator's guide to teaching literature. Contains a portion on realism in which *The Yearling* is discussed.

Lamar York, "Marjorie Kinnan Rawlings's Rivers," *Southern Literary Journal,* Spring 1977.

Historical Background

Michael Gannon, ed., *The New History of Florida.* Gainesville: University Press of Florida, 1996. Contains essays by various historians regarding the history of Florida from its original inhabitants to the present.

Andrew Sinclair, *Prohibition: The Era of Excess.* Boston: Atlantic Monthly Press, 1962. Provides a useful overview of the Prohibition era in the United States.

Index

Picture Credits

About the Author

Jennifer Keeley is a freelance writer who lives and works in Seattle, Washington. She graduated from Carleton College in 1996 with a degree in history and her teaching certificate. She has taught history and social studies in both the Seattle and Minneapolis public schools.